P9-BZR-981

ROMANTIC PATCHWORK & QUILTING

♥

By Ciba Vaughan

Photographs by Schecter Lee

Sedgewood® Press
New York, N.Y.

ACKNOWLEDGMENTS

Heartfelt thanks first, last, and always, to my family and friends. Their enthusiasm, support, and—most important—sense of humor, kept me patched together as I prepared the projects for this book. Special thanks, also, to a new friend, Heather Davis of Cambridge, Massachusetts, who cheerfully and expertly quilted the Filler Pattern Sampler pillow, Falling Timbers wall hanging, and Wanderer quilt in record time to help me meet a deadline.

Although most of the projects in this book were stitched from scraps or from yard goods available in any well-stocked quilting supply shop, a few of the designs were actually inspired by specific fabrics. These include the following: Flower Patch pillow, page 16: fabric by Concord Fabrics; *Broderie Perse* pillow, page 30: floral print by Kenmill Fabric; Lace Heart wall hanging, page 69: lace by Lace Country; Beautiful Borders projects, page 83: fabrics by VIP; Irish Chain weekend quilt, page 113: Coventry Collection fabrics by Hoffman; Hearts and Flowers crib quilt, page 122: floral print by Jay Yang Designs, Ltd.; Peaceful Star quilt, page 137: courtesy of Handblock, New York.

The wooden craft boxes framing Bow Tie designs on page 63 are from Sudberry House, and the moire wrapping papers featured in the Christmas chapter were supplied by Gordon Frazier.

Finally, I'm especially grateful to the supportive, patient staff of Sedgewood Press, and to designer Remo Cosentino, photographer Schecter Lee, and illustrator Gary Tong for their generous efforts on behalf of *Romantic Patchwork and Quilting*.

For Sedgewood® Press:
Director: Elizabeth P. Rice
Editorial Project Manager: Barbara Machtiger
Project Editor: Sydne Matus
Production Manager: Bill Rose
Design: Remo Cosentino/Bookgraphics
Prop Stylist: Diane Wagner

Copyright © 1989 by Ciba Vaughan. All rights reserved.
Distributed by Meredith Corporation, Des Moines, Iowa
ISBN: 0-696-02313-X
Library of Congress Catalog Card Number: 88-061385
Printed in the United States of America
10   9   8   7   6   5   4   3   3   2

CONTENTS

INTRODUCTION

As we approach the final decade of the twentieth century, it is intriguing to note that the age-old crafts of patchwork and quilting are nearly as popular today as they were in the early days of the Republic, more than two hundred years ago. Quilting shops are thriving in small towns, large cities, and suburban shopping malls all over the country, and quilting clubs, circles, guilds, and societies continue to proliferate, attracting members of every age and level of experience.

The American Museum of Quilts and Textiles was established in San José, California, in 1976, as part of the American Bicentennial celebration. In 1988, the New England Quilt Museum opened in Lowell, Massachusetts. These are two of the first — but likely not the last — museums in the country devoted exclusively to the preservation, documentation, appreciation, and exposition of quilts, both antique and contemporary.

Like the nation itself, this most American of crafts has undergone considerable changes over the last two hundred years. Although there are still women who learned to quilt at a mother's or grandmother's knee (as their ancestors did in days gone by), many more women today have had no home-based experience in quilting at all. Now, as adults, they are learning to quilt from books, in classes, or from their friends and contemporaries. Thus a whole new group of women — and, increasingly, men — come to quilting with neither expectations nor preconceptions about the process. One welcome result of this burgeoning interest among non-traditionally trained quilters is an influx of new ideas and a new sense of possibilities, both of which keep the craft and art of quilting alive and exciting. In classes and workshops all across the country, traditional designs and techniques are being preserved and shared, at the same time that new designs and techniques are springing to life. Quilters are rediscovering the fascination of novelty techniques like crazy patchwork and *Broderie Perse*, experimenting with non-traditional fabrics and patterns, and exploring personal design choices. And today, in the best melting-pot tradition of this country, new arrivals from all over the world bring with them new stitchery techniques, sensibilities, and preferences for colors and patterns that further expand and enrich the existing American patchwork vocabulary.

This book includes a selection of patterns and projects, both large and small, designed to entice the novice and delight the experienced quilter as well. Most are traditional patterns interpreted in a contemporary fashion, with a few helpful hints to speed your progress and expand your horizons.

The opening chapter is a kind of patchwork sampler. It includes a spill of pillow designs using assorted techniques that offer you an opportunity to hone your piecing, appliqué, and quilting skills before you proceed to some of the more complex projects in succeeding chapters.

Chapter II offers a choice of small gifts to make for family and friends (or to keep for yourself). All are reasonably quick to stitch and certain to please.

In Chapter III you'll find a potpourri of projects for the home, and, for those who always have an eye on Christmas, there's a sparkling assortment of tree trim and holiday accessories in Chapter IV. Finally, in Chapter V, I've included a select group of very special quilts and coverlets. Some are new, a few are old — all are worthy of your very best efforts.

This collection reflects my own penchant for the romantic side of patchwork: floral fabrics, pastel colors, and quilts or other designs with a sentimental history. And since I'm a fabric addict, constitutionally unable to discard a single scrap of fabric once it crosses the threshold of my workroom, you will also find a number of scrap-fabric projects. These offer delightful ways to use up all those odds and ends of fabric you may have been squirreling away for years.

Remember that each of the designs in this book awaits your own personal touch. Select a project that strikes your fancy, then interpret it in the colors and fabrics you favor. Whatever your choices, I hope that stitching the projects in this book will afford you a small portion of the pleasure I had in assembling them.

One final note: Please take a moment to review the information on patchwork terms and techniques that follows. Familiarity with this material will make the instructions for individual projects that much easier to follow.

PATCHWORK BASICS: A Glossary of Terms, Tools, and Techniques

Appliqué. The technique of creating a design by cutting shapes from one or more pieces of fabric and stitching these shapes by hand or machine to a background piece of fabric.

Backing. The piece of fabric used on the underside of a patchwork design. The backing fabric can be plain or fancy, a solid color or a print, depending on your preference. I prefer to use all-cotton backing fabrics in general, and I'm partial to muslin in particular. The latter is available in generous widths (up to 88 inches), making it unnecessary to piece backings except for the largest quilts. Many quilters like to use sheets for quilt backing for the same reason.

If you choose fabric other than extra-wide muslin, you may find it necessary to piece the backing for any project wider than 45 inches. Piece the backing in whichever way makes the most sense economically and aesthetically, given your choice of fabric. *Always* preshrink fabric before cutting and piecing.

Hint: I usually cut backing fabric at least 2 inches larger than the dimensions called for in the directions to allow for possible "shrinkage" when the project is quilted. Extra fabric can be trimmed away when the quilting is completed.

Basting. Long, loose running stitches used to secure 2 pieces of fabric together before stitching by hand or machine. Basting stitches are also used to secure the 3 layers of a quilt together (top, batting, and backing) before quilting. Basting stitches are always removed from the finished project.

Batting. The layer of stuffing sandwiched between the patchwork top and the backing. Batting makes the quilt warm and puffy. Most quilt batting is made of either cotton or polyester or a combination of the two, and it is available in thicknesses ranging from $1/8$ inch to as much as 2 inches or more. In general, the thicker the batting, the more difficult it is to quilt. For most of the projects in this book, $1/4$- to $1/2$-inch batting should be about right, but you will want to experiment with different materials and thicknesses to discover what suits you best.

Like the backing fabric, batting should be cut about 2 inches larger all around than the pieced top, as it may "shrink" somewhat during the quilting process.

Block. Refers to a single unit of a pieced or appliquéd patchwork design. Also called a *square*. A number of blocks are usually sewn together to make a complete quilt top.

Borders. Strips of fabric used to frame a quilt top. Borders may be wide or narrow, cut from matching or contrasting fabric. I usually cut the borders for large projects — such as quilts — before cutting other pattern pieces from the same fabric, to avoid having to piece the borders together from scraps. I also make it a point to cut the border strips 2 or 3 inches longer than called for in the directions, just to be on the safe side.

Enlarging Patterns. Most of the patterns in this book are printed full size. However, in a few cases, where patterns were too large for the page, the designs appear on a grid in which 1 square equals 1 inch (or, occasionally, some other measurement such as "1 square equals 2 inches"). To enlarge these patterns, simply draw a grid of squares in the size indicated (e.g., 1-inch squares) on a sheet of paper. Then, using a light pencil, copy the elements of the pattern from the book page to the paper, enlarging the design line by line, 1 square at a time.

Fabrics. All fabric yardage estimates in this book are based on 45-inch-wide fabric, unless otherwise specified. Occasionally I have used decorator chintzes and slipcover fabrics for some projects, and these often come in wider widths (56 to 72 inches wide). If you choose to work with similar materials for a given project, adjust fabric requirements in the materials list accordingly.

Most of the fabrics used in patchwork are cotton and cotton blends. These fabrics should *always* be washed and preshrunk before you begin to cut out the pieces for a project. Nothing is more heartbreaking than a beautifully finished quilt that shrinks out of shape the first time it is washed or one that includes patches of a pretty novelty print that bleeds or fades. Don't take the risk; it isn't worth it. I speak from bitter experience!

Fabric Markers. Some sort of fabric marker is essential for tracing templates onto fabric, marking stitching lines, and other tasks involved in the creation of a patchwork design.

Personally, I prefer to use quilter's or tailor's chalk, or one of the new "disappearing" pens (the kind that makes a bright purple line on cotton fabrics; the line lasts for about 8 hours and then — miraculously — fades away). Whatever marking method you choose, *always* test the marker on a scrap of every fabric you plan to use for a given project, to make sure that it will not leave a lasting mark. I keep a selection of different markers on hand, since I find that some work better on some fabrics than on others.

Finishing. The way in which a particular piece of patchwork is made into a completed project — such as a quilt or pillow top. (For more information on finishing, turn to pages 40–45.)

Mitering. The diagonal joining of 2 edges at a corner. Mitering gives quilt borders a neat, symmetrical finish.

Patchwork. The term for designs made from pieces of fabric sewn together. Piecing and appliqué are both forms of patchwork, as I use the term in this book.

Piecing, or Pieced Work. The seaming together by hand or machine of pieces of fabric — usually geometric shapes — in a certain arrangement to create a design. Most of the patchwork designs in this book are pieced.

In piecing any patchwork pattern, study the design first to determine the order in which the pieces are sewn together. Always begin by piecing the smallest units first, and then stitch these together to form larger units. Always press the seams on each unit before proceeding to the next step.

Pressing Patchwork. In traditional patchwork, seams are always pressed in one direction (usually toward the darker fabric), never open. This serves to strengthen the seams; it also makes it easier to match seams accurately and reduces bulk when you piece complex patterns.

However, for simple designs, I often choose to press the seams open, particularly when I plan to machine quilt a design "in the ditch" (along the seam lines).

In the end, whether you decide to be a purist and press patchwork seams to the side, or occasionally opt to press them open, it is really a matter of personal choice. But you should *always* press them before proceeding from one step to the next. Pressing seam lines keeps them crisp and even and ensures that the finished patchwork block will lie flat and smooth. Whichever method you prefer, pressing should be consistent from block to block on any given project.

Quilting. Stitching together the 3 layers of the quilt "sandwich" (patchwork top, batting, and backing fabric).

Quilting Patterns. The designs the quilting stitches make on the surface of the quilt.

Sashes, or Lattice Strips. The narrow pieces of fabric used to frame each patchwork block and to join the blocks together to form a quilt top.

Seam Allowances. The distance between the cut edge of a piece of fabric and the stitching line. All seam allowances in this book are gauged at ¼ inch wide unless otherwise specified in the directions.

Sewing Equipment. The basic tools for patchwork and quilting are the staples of any sewing project: a good, well-oiled sewing machine, sharp scissors, a metal-edged ruler and an accurately calibrated yardstick, plus assorted pins, needles, and threads. Most professional stitchers also insist on a thimble, but I must admit that I rarely use one myself except when I'm quilting on very heavy fabrics or thick batting.

Template. A full-size cardboard or plastic pattern shape used to trace the pattern pieces of a patchwork design onto fabric. Templates for pieced patchwork are usually traced onto the wrong side of the fabric, while templates for appliqué designs are usually traced onto the right side of the fabric.

Templates are usually cut from lightweight, stiff cardboard or plastic (the kind salvaged from coffee-can lids). However, most fabric stores sell packages of clear acrylic sheets printed with 1-inch grids. These sheets are a bit expensive, but they make accurate cutting and positioning of templates much easier.

Top. The term usually used to refer to a pieced or appliquéd patchwork design before it has been assembled with batting and backing to make a quilt.

A Sampler of Patchwork Pillows

Learn the ABC's of patchwork or perfect your piecing, appliqué, and quilting skills as you stitch any of the dozen different pillow designs in this chapter.

Pieced Patchwork

Pieced work — the stitching together of pieces of fabric in a certain arrangement to create a design — is perhaps the most familiar and versatile form of patchwork. It is also the technique used for most of the projects in this book.

SQUARES AND TRIANGLES: SISTER'S CHOICE

Piecing the Sister's Choice block — a simple arrangement of squares and triangles — offers a quick refresher course in basic piecing techniques. The steps explained in detail in the directions that follow will be referred to again and again in the directions for other projects in the book.

Just for fun, we've pieced the Sister's Choice block in 3 different fabric combinations, as a visual reminder that the same pattern can produce dramatically different results when pieced in different colors and materials. Directions for the simple pink and white version of the pattern block follow. The finished pillow is about 18 × 18 inches square.

Materials
⅓ yard pink print fabric
½ yard white fabric for pieced top and pillow backing
18½-inch square lightweight muslin for lining pattern block
18½-inch square lightweight batting
fiber fill or 18-inch square purchased pillow form
cardboard or plastic for templates

Directions
Note: All pattern pieces and measurements include ¼-inch seam allowances.

1. Preshrink all fabrics.

2. Trace pattern pieces (*A*) and (*B*), on page 15, and transfer to cardboard or plastic for templates. (See page 9 for details on templates.)

3. Trace around the templates on the *wrong* side of the fabric and cut the following pieces:

from white fabric:
    (*A*) 8 squares
    (*B*) 8 triangles

from pink fabric:
    (*A*) 9 squares
    (*B*) 8 triangles

for borders:
    2 strips, each 2 × 15½ inches
    2 strips, each 2 × 18½ inches

4. With right sides facing, pin and stitch one pink triangle (*B*) and one white triangle (*B*) together along the diagonal, using ¼-inch seams. Stitch seam and

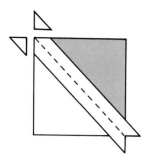

Figure 1. Piece together triangles into a square and trim points

press square. Trim the points on the triangles (see Figure 1). Piece a total of 8 squares from pink and white triangles.

5. Next, arrange the pink squares, white squares, and pieced squares in 5 rows of 5 squares each, following the assembly diagram in Figure 2.

6. Piece squares in each row together to form 1 row of pattern. Then stitch all 5 rows together to complete 1 pattern block. Use ¼-inch seams throughout. Press the block carefully.

To Assemble the Pillow Top:

1. Pin and stitch one 2 × 15½-inch border strip to each side of the pieced block. Press seams toward borders and trim length of strips if necessary. Then pin and stitch one 2 × 18½-inch strip to the top and one to the bottom of block; trim ends and press seams.

2. Cut squares of batting and muslin to size (about 18½ inches square). Layer muslin, batting, and pieced top together and baste through all 3 layers.

3. Quilt the pillow top as desired. (This pillow top is outline-quilted along seam lines.) For quilting instructions, see page 37.

4. Back quilted pillow top with a matching square of fabric. Stitch around 4 corners and 3 sides, trim corners, turn and press. Stuff pillow with fiber fill and slip-stitch the opening closed.

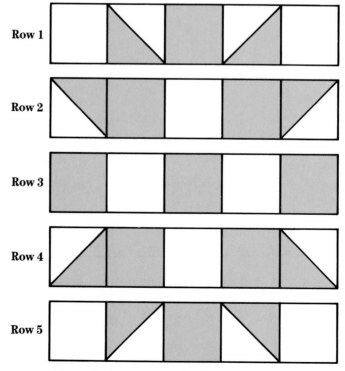

Figure 2. Assembly diagram for Sister's Choice quilt

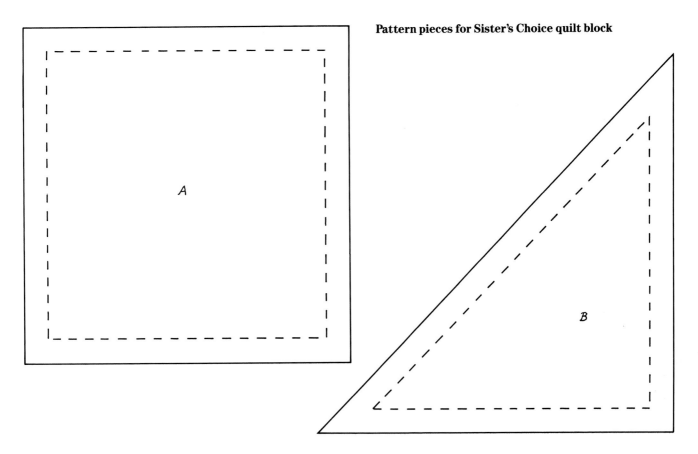

Pattern pieces for Sister's Choice quilt block

CENTERED MOTIFS: FLOWER PATCH DESIGN

The charming Flower Patch pillow on the next page illustrates the advantage of using see-through plastic templates (rather than cardboard or opaque plastic shapes) when working with certain fabrics. Fabrics with large or widely scattered prints or with very distinct motifs can be wonderfully dramatic in pieced patchwork, but only if you can position the templates to take maximum advantage of the fabric design when tracing and cutting pattern pieces. (See page 9 for more on clear plastic templates.) Use clear plastic or acrylic templates whenever you need to cut fabric pieces with centered motifs.

This Flower Patch design began as a conventional 9-patch pattern (9 same-size squares arranged in 3 rows of 3 squares each). Having settled on a fabric, I chose to make the center square of the design larger, to accommodate a large spray of blossoms, and made the corner squares correspondingly smaller, to display individual flowers. The remaining white "squares" were recast as rectangles to complete the pattern block.

Step-by-step instructions for the 10½-inch Flower Patch pillow pictured follow, but use these only as guidelines for piecing a patchwork design from your own favorite flower print fabric. Adjust the dimensions of the pattern pieces to suit the size of motifs on the fabric of your choice.

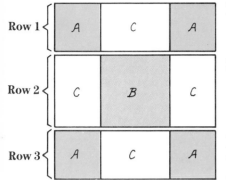

Row 1 { A | C | A

Row 2 { C | B | C

Row 3 { A | C | A

Figure 1. Assembly diagram for Flower Patch block

Materials

½ yard floral or other print fabric for pieced top and 2-inch-wide ruffle
⅓ yard white or contrasting fabric for pieced top and backing
2⅔ yards 1½-inch eyelet lace for inner ruffle
1⅓ yards fabric-covered cording for trim
11 × 11-inch square of lightweight muslin
11 × 11-inch square of lightweight batting
polyester fiber fill
clear plastic for templates

Directions

Note: All pattern pieces and measurements include ¼-inch seam allowances.

1. Measure and cut the following template shapes from clear plastic:
    (*A*) 3½ × 3½-inch square
    (*B*) 5 × 5-inch square
    (*C*) 3½ × 5-inch rectangle

2. Trace around templates on the *wrong* side of the fabric, centering motifs on each pattern piece, and cut the following pieces:

from print fabric:
    (*A*) 4 small squares
    (*B*) 1 large square

from white fabric:
  (C) 4 rectangles

3. Arrange the squares and rectangles in 3 rows of 3 pieces each (see Figure 1, opposite page). Pin and stitch the pieces in each row together, using ¼-inch seams throughout. Press seams. Then pin and stitch the 3 rows together to form the pillow top.

To Assemble the Pillow:

1. Cut matching pieces of batting and muslin to size (approximately 11 × 11 inches). Layer and baste the muslin lining, batting, and pieced top together and quilt around pieces ¼ inch inside seam lines.

2. Add fabric-covered cording and a double ruffle of eyelet lace and print fabric to pillow top (see pages 41–42 for ruffle and cording instructions).

3. Back quilted pillow top with a matching square of white fabric, stitch around 4 corners and 3 sides, trim corners, turn, and press. Stuff pillow with fiber fill and slip-stitch the opening closed.

STRIP PIECING: CHECKERBOARD SQUARES

Strip piecing is a wonderfully timesaving technique that eliminates the need to cut and piece individual squares into pattern blocks. Instead, you stitch long strips of fabric together and then cut these strips into rows of already-pieced

squares, which are then rearranged and stitched together to form complete pattern blocks. Several projects in this book make use of this quick-and-easy technique, but success depends entirely on careful marking and precise cutting. Practice on this 15-inch-square checkered block design to familiarize yourself with the technique.

Materials

½ yard *each* of a print and a solid fabric for pieced top and backing
16-inch square of lightweight muslin
16-inch square of batting
polyester fiber fill
1¾ yards contrasting fabric-covered cording
metal-edged ruler or yardstick

Directions

Note: All measurements include ¼-inch seam allowances.

1. Cut 3 strips of print fabric, each 3 × 18 inches. Cut 3 matching strips of coordinating, solid-color fabric.

2. Pin and stitch the 6 strips together as shown in Figure 1, below. Press.

3. Lay the pieced strips out on a flat surface. Using a sharp pencil or fabric marker and the metal-edged ruler or yardstick, carefully draw lines across the pieced strips, dividing the strip-pieced fabric into six 3-inch-wide strips. See Figure 1.

4. Cut the strips apart. Reverse the second, fourth, and sixth strips, and, with right sides facing, re-pin all 6 strips together to form the checkered block pattern shown in Figure 2. Match corners carefully where seams meet, to keep the pattern crisp and sharp. Stitch strips together and press seams.

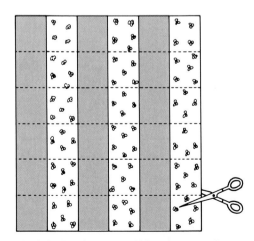

**Figure 1. Stitch print and solid strips together.
Cut into new strips of alternating squares.**

Figure 2. Assembling strip-pieced units to form Checkerboard pattern.

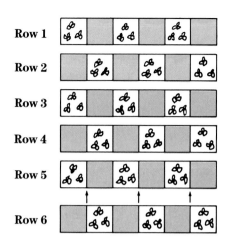

Row 1

Row 2

Row 3

Row 4

Row 5

Row 6

5. Layer the pieced top together with batting and muslin; quilt as desired (see page 37). Finish pillow top with cording. (See page 41 for details on cording.)

6. Back the quilted pillow top with a matching square of solid fabric. Stitch around 4 corners and 3 sides. Trim seams, turn, press, stuff, and slip-stitch fourth side closed.

PRESSED PIECING: LOG CABIN DESIGNS

One traditional method of assembling Log Cabin pattern blocks, the one used for projects in this book, is called pressed piecing. It is a combination of piecing and appliqué, and is particularly useful when you're working with hard-to-handle fabrics or piecing fabrics of different textures (such as silks and velvets) together.

In the pressed piecing method, the center square of the Log Cabin block is basted to a thin muslin lining square. Logs of light and dark fabrics in graduated lengths are then stitched in sequence around the center square, one by one. Each strip is pressed in place before the next log is added.

The size of the center square plus the width and number of fabric logs surrounding it determine the size of the basic block. The way in which groups of blocks are then pieced together determines the overall Log Cabin pattern. There are many Log Cabin arrangements; three are pictured on page 20, along with a ruffled accent pillow composed of a single, basic Log Cabin square.

ONE-BLOCK LOG CABIN PILLOW

Materials

½ yard floral print for block center, backing, and ruffle
   scraps of 3 light (peach, yellow, medium-pink) and 3 dark (light-blue, green, medium-blue) fabrics for logs
12-inch square of muslin for lining
fiber fill
pencil and ruler

Directions

Note: All measurements include ¼-inch seam allowance.

1. When you cut fabric strips for the Log Cabin block, it is important to cut all strips exactly the same *width* — in this case 1¾ inches wide. (I generally find it easiest to cut long strips of the proper width from each fabric to be used, and then cut the strips into appropriate lengths as each block is being constructed.)

2. For the basic Log Cabin block, you will need to cut the following pieces:

from floral print:
    (A) one 3½ × 3½-inch square

from 1¾-inch-wide strips of fabric, cut logs in the following lengths:
    peach: (B) 3½ inches and (C) 4¾ inches
    light-blue: (D) 4¾ inches and (E) 6 inches
    yellow: (F) 6 inches and (G) 7¼ inches
    green: (H) 7¼ inches and (I) 8½ inches
    medium-pink: (J) 8½ inches and (K) 9¾ inches
    medium-blue: (L) 9¾ inches and (M) 11 inches

To Assemble the Log Cabin Block:

1. Using a pencil and ruler, lightly mark the muslin square diagonally from corner to corner to locate the center and to aid in keeping the logs square as you construct the block. Center and baste the flowered square piece (A) in the exact center of the muslin lining square.

2. With right sides facing, lay log (B) along one side of (A). Pin and stitch (B) in place with ¼-inch seam. See Figure 1. Press.

3. Next, pin and stitch log (C) to (A)–(B) block, as shown in Figure 2. Press.

4. Continue adding fabric logs in order, pieces (D) through (M), pressing each strip flat before adding the next, until you have completed the Log Cabin block (see Figure 3). Note that 2 light-colored logs are followed by 2 dark-colored logs, followed by 2 light-colored logs, and so on around the square, creating dark and light diagonal halves to the block.

To Finish the Pillow:

1. Log Cabin designs constructed in the pressed piecing method usually are not quilted, but if you like, you can outline quilt each strip about ³⁄₁₆ inch in from the seam lines.

2. Make a 3-inch-wide ruffle of print fabric and baste it to the pieced pillow front (see page 42 for details on ruffles).

3. Back the pillow with matching or contrasting fabric. Stitch around 4 corners and 3 sides. Trim corners, turn, and press. Stuff pillow with fiber fill and slip-stitch fourth side closed.

**Assembly Diagrams
for Log Cabin Block**

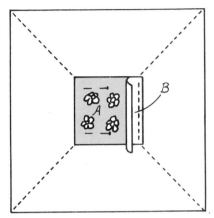

Figure 1. Sew Log (B) to center square (A)

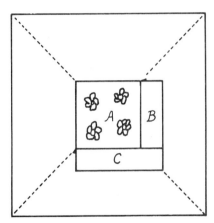

Figure 2. Add log (C) to block (A)(B)

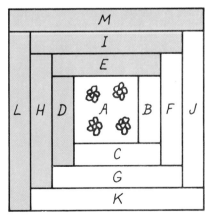

Figure 3. Completed Log Cabin block

21

FOUR-BLOCK LOG CABIN PILLOWS

The 3 larger pillows pictured on page 20 and diagrammed at right illustrate 3 traditional arrangements for pieced Log Cabin blocks. Blocks for these pillows are constructed the same way as the single block described on pages 19–21, but the center squares and log strips are smaller. Each single block measures 8 × 8 inches, and the finished pillows each measure 16 inches square.

Materials (for each pillow)

½ yard print fabric for center square, cording, and backing
⅛ yard *each* of 3 light and 3 dark fabrics for logs
¼ yard lightweight muslin for block linings
fiber fill
2 yards cotton cording

Directions

Note: All measurements include ¼-inch seam allowances.

1. For *each* Log Cabin square, cut the following pieces:

from muslin:
    one 8½ × 8½-inch square

from print fabric:
    (A) one 2½ × 2½-inch square

from 1¼-inch-wide strips of fabric, cut logs in the following lengths:
    peach: (B) 2½ inches and (C) 3¼ inches
    light-blue: (D) 3¼ inches and (E) 4 inches
    yellow: (F) 4 inches and (G) 4¾ inches
    green: (H) 4¾ inches and (I) 5½ inches
    medium-pink: (J) 5½ inches and (K) 6¼ inches
    medium-blue: (L) 6¼ inches and (M) 7 inches

2. Construct 4 Log Cabin squares for each pillow top, following directions for One-Block Log Cabin Pillow, pages 19–21.

To Assemble the Pillow Tops:

1. For the Light and Dark pattern, pin and stitch 4 blocks together as shown in Figure 4.

2. For the Straight Furrow pillow top, pin and stitch 4 blocks together as shown in Figure 5.

3. For the Pinwheel pattern, pin and stitch 4 blocks together as shown in Figure 6.

4. Trim pillow tops with fabric-covered cording, if desired (see page 41). Then back, stitch, turn and stuff pillows. Slip-stitch fourth side of each pillow closed.

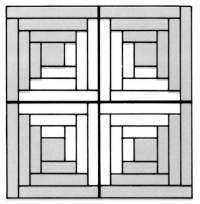

Figure 4. Light and Dark

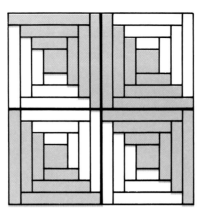

Figure 5. Straight Furrow

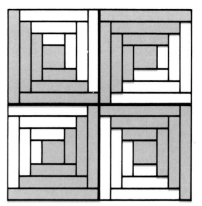

Figure 6. Pinwheel

The Art of Appliqué

Appliqué entails shapes cut from one or more pieces of fabric and stitched on top of a background fabric to form a design. As in pieced work, appliqué designs can be stitched by hand or machine, and can be elaborate or simple, elegant or downright folksy, depending on the complexity of the design, the materials used, and the skill of the stitcher.

TRADITIONAL APPLIQUÉ: FLORAL WREATH DESIGN

The 15-inch-square Floral Wreath pillow pictured on page 25 is an adaptation of a traditional appliqué pattern and is a good project on which to hone your basic appliqué skills. Cut the stylized blossoms from scraps of different calico prints or from solid-color fabrics, as you prefer.

Materials

small amounts of 5 different print or solid-color fabrics for flowers, plus scraps
    of gold for flower centers
¼ yard green fabric for leaves and stems
½ yard white fabric for background square and pillow back
½ yard contrasting fabric for ruffle
2 yards fabric-covered cording for trim (optional)
cardboard or plastic for templates

Directions

To Prepare Background Square:

1. Cut a 15½-inch square of white fabric for background.

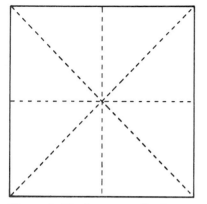

Figure 1. Mark center of background square

2. To mark the center of square and to aid in positioning appliqué pieces, press the square in half vertically, horizontally, and diagonally, as shown in Figure 1.

3. Using a compass or a plate of the appropriate size, trace an 8-inch circle on the center of the background fabric. Use a light pencil or a "disappearing" marker to outline the circle. (See note on fabric markers, page 8.)

To Trace and Cut Appliqué Shapes:

1. Trace patterns for the blossom, leaf, and flower center (page 28) and make a template for each shape. (Patterns do *not* include seam allowances.)

2. Unlike the procedure for pieced patchwork, templates for appliqués are traced on the *right* side of the fabric, and the traced line is the *stitching* line, not the cutting line. When tracing templates on fabric, leave at least a ½-inch space between each shape to accommodate the ¼-inch seam allowance on each piece. Seam allowances are added when the shapes are cut out.

3. Trace and cut out 5 blossoms (from different print or solid-color fabrics). Also trace and cut out 5 gold flower centers and 15 green leaves. For hand appliqué, leave ¼-inch seam allowance when cutting around each shape (see Figure 2); omit seam allowances for machine appliqué.

4. Fold the remaining green fabric on the diagonal and cut out 5 bias strips for wreath stems, each ½ × 5 inches. (Cut stems only ¼ inch wide for machine appliqué). For tips on cutting bias strips, see page 43.

To Prepare Shapes for Appliqué:

1. Trim corners and clip curved edges of each appliqué shape perpendicular to, and just short of, the traced stitching line.

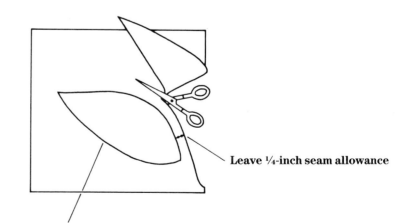

Leave ¼-inch seam allowance

Traced stitching line

Figure 2. Cut out shapes for hand appliqué

2. You can either baste the turned-under seam allowance on appliqué shapes before pinning them in place, or — a much faster method, but one that requires some practice — use the tip of your finger or needle to coax under the seam allowance as you stitch each appliqué in place. You may want to baste the turned-under seam allowances on shapes that are fairly regular and smooth-sided, and use the tip-of-the-needle method on more irregular shapes. Use either method or both — whatever seems most comfortable. In any case, there is no need to turn under the seam allowance on portions of the appliqué that will be overlapped by other shapes. In fact, turning under these segments of seam allowance adds bulk that is undesirable, especially for designs that will be quilted. (See To Quilt Appliqué Designs, page 28.)

3. On bias-cut stems, press under ¼-inch seam allowances along each edge of strip for hand appliqué, but do not turn under seam allowances at the ends of the strip.

To Position Appliqués on Background Fabric:

1. Using the creased lines and traced circle as guides, lay out all pattern pieces, as shown in Figure 3.

2. Pin the stems in place, covering the traced outlines of the circle. Trim the ends of each stem section where blossoms overlap.

Figure 3. Assembly diagram for Floral Wreath design

To Stitch Appliqués in Place:

1. Appliqué the shapes in sequence: background pieces first, then foreground shapes. Stitch stems first, and then leaves. Stitch centers to flowers, then stitch flowers in place.

2. Using thread that matches the appliqué shape, stitch each piece in place with tiny slip stitches, whipstitches, or running stitches. See Figures 4a, 4b, and 4c. (Traditionally, appliqué shapes were often stitched in place with decorative buttonhole stitches worked with matching or contrasting embroidery floss; use this method of appliqué if you prefer. See Figure 4d.)

3. For machine appliqué, trim shapes to stitching line (no seam allowance) and tack appliqués to the background fabric with basting stitches or light dabs of fabric glue. Next, using matching thread and a straight stitch, sew slowly and carefully all the way around each shape, just inside the cutting line. Make sure that each shape lies flat and smooth against the background fabric. Then, outline each appliqué shape with a close zigzag satin stitch in matching or contrasting thread.

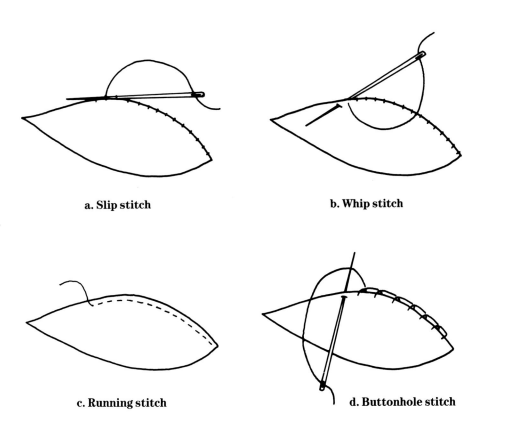

a. Slip stitch

b. Whip stitch

c. Running stitch

d. Buttonhole stitch

Figure 4. Appliqué stitches

To Quilt Appliqué Designs:

1. Many appliqué designs are not quilted, particularly on small blocks. But if you plan to quilt the finished design, turn the completed appliqué to the *wrong* side and carefully cut away the background fabric beneath each appliquéd shape. Take special pains not to cut into the appliqué fabric itself. Leave between ⅛- and ¼-inch seam allowance beyond each line of stitching so that appliqué remains fastened securely to the background fabric. (This is an optional step, but it does reduce bulk from the overlapping layers of fabric, and also helps to eliminate puckers in the completed design.)

2. Quilt the pattern as desired. For appliqué designs, usually the most successful choice is simple outline quilting ¼ inch beyond the stitching lines around each shape. For details on quilting and quilting stitches, see page 37.

To Finish the Pillow:

Pin and stitch a row of cording and a 4-inch-wide ruffle to pillow top, as explained on pages 41–42. Back with matching fabric. Stitch around 4 corners and 3 sides. Trim corners, turn the pillow right side out and press. Stuff with fiber fill and slip-stitch closed.

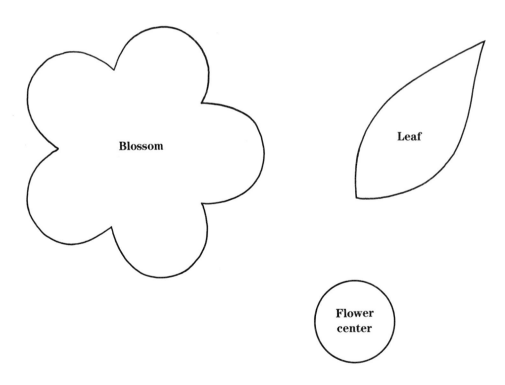

Pattern pieces for appliquéd Floral Wreath design

BRODERIE PERSE: VASE OF FLOWERS

Broderie Perse patchwork, the appliqué of motifs cut from chintz or other patterned fabric onto a plain background, was popular with many American quilters throughout the nineteenth century. One advantage of this technique is that it enables you to compose wonderfully elaborate, colorful designs with relative ease. Flower bouquets and garlands can be cut from scraps of a single fabric, rather than from as many as a dozen different fabrics, as would be necessary for an equally complex design using more traditional appliqué techniques. Instead of composing a rose petal by separate petal, you simply clip one entire flower from a piece of printed chintz, arrange it on the background fabric and stitch it in place.

As in traditional appliqué, chintz cutouts can be hand appliquéd with a whipstitch, slip stitch, or running stitch, or with decorative embroidery such as the buttonhole stitch. Pieces can also be appliquéd by machine, using a narrow zigzag satin stitch. For machine appliqué, omit seam allowance.

In *Broderie Perse* designs, the look and shape of the design depends on the print fabric you select, which motifs you cut out, and the way in which you arrange them on the background fabric, rather than on a pattern that is traced and reproduced exactly. Using the pillow top pictured on the next page as inspiration, create your own Vase of Flowers design from fabrics of your choice.

Materials
¼ to ½ yard (approximately) floral print chintz for appliqués
½ yard white cotton fabric for pillow front and back
½ yard blue print fabric for vase and for pillow ruffle
2 yards contrasting fabric-covered cording or piping
fiber fill

Directions
1. Cut a 16 × 16-inch square of white fabric and press in half diagonally to mark the center of the square and to assist in the proper positioning of the appliqués (see pages 23–24).

2. From a 6½-inch square of blue print fabric, cut out a vase shape freehand (or enlarge and trace the shape that appears in Figure 1 on page 31). Add ¼-inch seam allowance.

3. Turn under seam allowance on vase, and baste; position and pin vase on background fabric.

4. Cut out a selection of blossoms and leaves from chintz fabric, leaving a ⅛- to 3/16-inch seam allowance around each piece. Cut away extraneous parts of the design — narrow vines, tendrils, small buds, and so on. Clip curves and corners and clip into seam allowance right up to the edge of the motif, as described for traditional appliqué (see pages 24–26).

5. Position blossoms and leaves in a bouquet atop the vase, adding, subtracting, and rearranging shapes until you're pleased with the design. Tack each piece to the background fabric with a single pin so you can keep track of the arrangement.

6. Carefully clip away excess fabric where shapes overlap, then stitch the motifs in place. Begin with background shapes and work toward the foreground. Follow directions for stitching appliqués on page 27.

To Finish the Pillow:

Add a row of cording or piping and a 3-inch ruffle of the blue print fabric (see pages 41–42 for details on cording and ruffles). Back the pillow with a matching square of white fabric. Stitch around 4 corners and 3 sides, trim corners, turn and press. Stuff pillow with fiber fill and slip-stitch fourth side closed.

Figure 1. Assembly diagram for Vase of Flowers appliqué

Special Techniques

There are literally dozens of different special techniques to explore once you get beyond the basics of patchwork and quilting. Two techniques that showcase elegant fabrics and nicely complement the current rage for all things Victorian are crazy patchwork and lace appliqué.

CRAZY PATCHWORK PILLOW

Crazy patchwork—a passion among Victorian-era quilters from about 1880 to the turn of the century—is really a form of the pressed piecing technique used to stitch the Log Cabin squares on pages 19–22. It consists of a random arrangement of odd-shaped fabric scraps stitched to a muslin base. The fabric shapes are cut from a wide variety of materials, often including silks, ribbons, velvets, and the like. Once stitched in place, crazy patchwork quilts were often embellished with elaborate embroidery in varicolored threads but, like Log Cabin designs, they were rarely quilted.

Pictured here is a contemporary version of crazy patchwork: a dainty pillow, pieced of "elegant" fabrics in pastel shades and embellished with smatterings of embroidery.

Note: On page 36, you will find a sampling of basic embroidery stitches with which to experiment. As your skill and sense of adventure expand, you will certainly want to consult specialized books on embroidery for more complex stitches and patterns.

Materials

13-inch square of muslin for lining
scraps of "elegant" fabrics (tie silks, satin lining fabrics, scraps from dress-weight fabrics, velveteens, ribbons, lace strips, and so on.)
½ yard contrasting fabric for backing and ruffle
1½ yards decorative cording
3 yards 1½-inch-wide lace
embroidery floss and pearl cotton in a variety of colors
fiber fill

Directions

1. Beginning in the upper left or right corner of the muslin square and working toward the center and bottom, arrange scraps of fabric in a pleasing random design, letting the shapes of your own fabric scraps dictate placement. Cover the lining fabric completely. The edges of the patches should extend slightly beyond the edges of the muslin lining square.

2. When all pieces are arranged to your satisfaction, pin and baste each shape in place, folding under the raw edges where one piece overlaps another and clipping away excess seam allowance as necessary.

3. Slip-stitch pieces to background fabric, taking tiny stitches through all layers of fabric to tack appliqué pieces to muslin.

4. When the square is finished, trim the edges of the patches back to the edge of the muslin square. Embellish all seams with embroidery stitches of your choice, using floss in a variety of colors. Refer to the color photo and to the stitch diagrams on page 36 for suggestions.

To Finish the Pillow:

1. Trim the pillow top with a row of decorative cording and a double ruffle of fabric and lace (see pages 41–42 for cording and ruffle instructions).

2. Back the pillow with contrasting fabric. Stitch around 4 corners and 3 sides. Trim corners, turn, and press. Stuff with fiber fill and slip-stitch fourth side closed.

LACE APPLIQUÉ DOILY PILLOW

Lace is a versatile material that adds a lavishly romantic touch to any project. But because it is often very fragile, lace requires special handling and extra-careful stitching for successful appliqué. Using a purchased lace doily or thrift-shop find and a yard or two of lace edging, you can practice the techniques of lace appliqué and complete this delightful little pillow in next to no time. By tinting the lace with commercial fabric dyes, you can create lace pillow tops — even whole lace quilts — in any color you choose.

Note: Most fabric dyes work best on all-cotton fabrics, so select your lace doily and trim accordingly.

Materials
1 cotton lace doily (crocheted doilies work particularly well for this project, offering an interesting contrast of pattern and texture)
1 square or rectangle of white or off-white fabric (for backing) at least 2 to 3 inches wider than outer dimensions of doily
1 matching square or rectangle of fabric for pillow back
matching pieces of muslin lining and batting
enough lace trim to frame the doily
enough fabric-covered cording to trim the pillow
embroidery floss in matching or contrasting colors
fiber fill
fabric dye in the color of your choice (optional)

Directions
1. Dye the doily using commercial fabric dye, following the instructions on the package. Include lace trim and fabric cording in the dye bath as well, for a color-coordinated pillow top. Rinse and dry all materials thoroughly before proceeding.

2. Press all materials. Press the doily carefully, smoothing the delicate lace shape into a perfectly flat, symmetrical pattern. A light spray of starch often makes lace more manageable for appliqué.

Embroidery Stitches

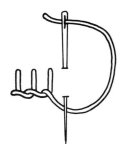

Buttonhole

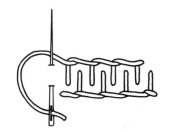

Double buttonhole

3. Arrange the doily on the center of backing fabric and pin in place. Working from the center of the doily out toward the edges, whipstitch the doily to the backing fabric with tiny, nearly invisible stitches. Use thread in a color to match the doily.

   You may tack as much or as little of the lace to the background fabric as you like, but the more stitches you take, the more stable the final appliqué will be. Keep in mind that lace is delicate and particularly subject to catches and snags, so the more carefully you stitch the doily in place, the longer the pillow is likely to last.

4. Cut layers of muslin lining and batting to size. Baste lining, batting, and appliquéd top together.

5. Appliqué a row of lace trim ⅜ inch inside the raw edges of the pillow top, framing the doily. If you like, embellish the pillow top with touches of embroidery to integrate the design (refer to the photo and this page for stitch suggestions).

6. Finally, stitch a row of matching cording around the perimeter of the pillow. (See page 41 for details on cording). Back the pillow top with matching or contrasting fabric. Stitch around 4 corners and 3 sides, trim corners, turn, and press. Stuff pillow and slip-stitch fourth side closed.

Chain

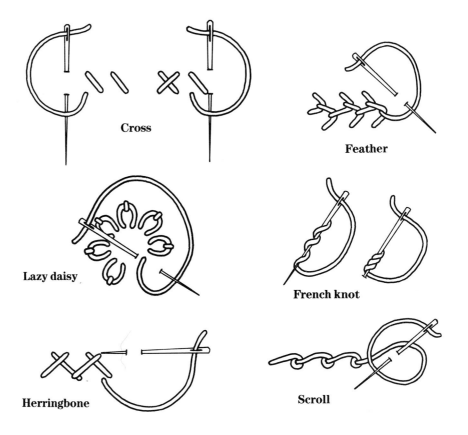

Cross

Feather

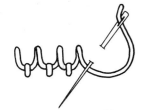

Parallel feather

Lazy daisy

French knot

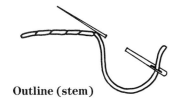

Outline (stem)

Herringbone

Scroll

Quilting

Quilting refers to the pattern of stitches taken through all 3 layers of the textile "sandwich": quilt top; filler or batting; and backing fabric. The quilting stitches are both practical and decorative. They are practical, because they strengthen the quilt and keep the batting from shifting and bunching, and decorative because they add a sculptured texture to the surface of the quilt. Quilting can be done either by hand or by machine.

QUILTING BASICS

There are essentially 4 types of traditional quilting:

Quilting "in the ditch": This simply means quilting in the seam lines around or between pattern pieces and/or quilt blocks. It is most successful on geometric pieced patterns, and is a particularly good choice if you want to machine quilt a project in a hurry.

Outline quilting: Also called echo quilting, this refers to lines of quilting stitches taken ⅛ to ¼ inch beyond the seam lines of a design. It is often used on appliqué patterns and on small pieced projects; I've used it frequently on projects in this book. Outline quilting is simple and effective, and eliminates the need to trace complex designs on the surface of the quilt.

Quilting motifs: These are individual designs, either geometric or pictorial — hearts, feathered wreaths, stars, flowers, and border designs — used to embellish individual squares and borders or other plain sections of a quilt or patchwork piece. You can trace quilting motif patterns from books, design your own, or purchase cardboard or plastic quilting templates from a local fabric shop.

Filler patterns: These are overall designs used to embellish large quilt blocks and borders, or repeated across an entire coverlet. A selection of 4 traditional filler patterns are shown on the quilted sampler pillow pictured on page 39.

Directions for the pillow follow a review of basic quilting instructions, which begins below. Whichever type of quilting you choose — "in the ditch," outline, motifs, or filler patterns — remember that the stitching should enhance, not overwhelm, the pieced or appliquéd designs.

Marking the Quilting Design

There is no need to mark guidelines for outline quilting on most projects, or for quilting "in the ditch," but other designs require some guidelines for the stitching.

In general, it is best to mark the quilting pattern on the quilt top before the "sandwich" is basted together. I suggest using either washable or "disappearing" fabric markers or quilter's chalk for marking, rather than pencil. Pencil marks, however lightly sketched, rarely disappear, even after repeated washings. A wide variety of suitable markers are available in quilting supply shops (see page 8). Always test your choice on a scrap of the quilt fabric first, before marking a whole design, to make sure that marker and fabric are compatible. For marking straight

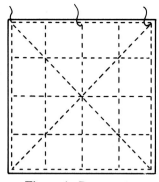

Figure 1. Baste quilt "sandwich" together

lines (parallel lines, diamonds, squares, etc.), use a good metal-edged ruler or yardstick and measure the distance between quilting lines carefully. Regularity of spacing enhances the beauty of the design.

For more complex designs, use homemade or purchased pattern templates.

Assembling the Quilt "Sandwich"

Piece backing fabric to size (see page 7). Spread out the backing fabric wrong side up on a flat surface (table or floor). Center the batting on the backing, then center the quilt top right side up on the batting. Smooth all 3 layers carefully from the center of the quilt out toward the edges. Any wrinkles or lumps not eliminated at this point will be stitched right into the quilt.

Pin and then baste the layers of the quilt together, working from the center out. Run lines of long basting stitches from the center of the quilt out to each corner, and then from side to side and top to bottom. If the project is large, run lines of basting horizontally and vertically across the surface at regular intervals (every 6 to 8 inches at least), to make sure that all 3 pieces are held firmly together and that the fabric and batting are evenly distributed (see Figure 1). Use white or light-colored thread for the basting; dark-colored thread often leaves a residue that is hard to eliminate even after the basting stitches have been removed.

Quilting Your Patchwork

To quilt your patchwork projects, use quilting thread (thread that has been treated to make it both strong and easy to draw through the layers of fabric and batting). Or use regular thread, if you prefer. Work with a strand of thread about 18 to 24 inches long — any longer and the thread tends to tangle. A size 7 or 8 quilting needle (known as a "between") is useful for taking small, even stitches, but by all means use whatever size needle feels comfortable to you.

While stitching, you can use a quilting frame, a large quilter's hoop or embroidery hoop, or you can simply hold the project in your lap and work without a frame or hoop at all. Do whichever is most comfortable, but remember that a frame or hoop does make it easier to maintain even spacing and tension in your quilting stitches.

To begin quilting, make a small knot in one end of the thread and draw the knotted end into a seam or draw the thread through the top of the fabric into the batting and give a little tug, so that the knot goes through the surface of the fabric and is buried in the batting.

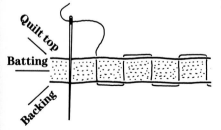

Figure 2. Quilting stitch

Quilting is simply a pattern of small, even running stitches taken through all 3 layers of the quilt "sandwich." Ideally, a line of quilting stitches should look the same on the front and the back of the quilt (see Figure 2). Tiny stitches are prized by quilt aficionados, but evenness and regularity of stitching are even more important than size to the appearance of the finished design.

To finish a row of quilting (or when you come to the end of a thread), make a

tiny knot in the thread and bury it beneath the surface of the quilt just as you did when you started.

Continue stitching until the quilting design is completed.

Tying a Quilt

Not all patchwork projects are quilted. Many are simply tied or tufted at strategic points across the surface of the design to hold the layers of fabric and batting together. Several projects in this book are handled in this way. Log Cabin patterns, for example, are traditionally tied at the corner of each block, rather than quilted.

To tie a quilt, simply take a small (¼-inch) running stitch through all 3 layers of fabric and batting, using a double strand of pearl cotton thread or crochet cotton for an attractive, sturdy stitch. Then, take a backstitch in exactly the same spot and bring the ends of the thread back to the same side of the quilt. Pull the stitch tight, tie the ends in a neat square knot and clip away excess thread. Repeat at regular intervals across the surface of the quilt.

FILLER PATTERN SAMPLER PILLOW

The finished pillow shown on the previous page measures 16 inches square. Each filler pattern is worked on one quadrant of the pillow top, using colored embroidery floss to highlight the designs. Worked in regular quilting thread, the quilted patterns would, of course, be more subtle.

Materials

17-inch squares of fabric for the pillow top and back
matching squares of batting and muslin
embroidery floss in your choice of colors

Directions

1. Trace a 16-inch square on the center of the pillow top fabric. Divide the square into 4 equal quadrants and mark the outlines of each quadrant with parallel lines ¼ inch apart. Enlarge the filler patterns shown in Figure 3 and trace one pattern in each quadrant.

2. Layer muslin, batting, and top together and baste, as described in the general directions on page 38. Quilt each design in colors of your choice, striving for even, regular stitches and even tension throughout.

3. Finish pillow top as desired (see below and pages 41–42).

Finishing Touches

After the piecing, appliqué, and quilting are done, quilts and other projects can be finished in a number of ways. Here are a few tips and techniques for completing the projects in this book.

Finishing Patchwork Pillows

Pillows can simply be backed with a matching or contrasting piece of fabric, or finished more elaborately with a trim of cording and/or ruffles.

Each square equals 1 inch

Upper left quadrant   **Upper right quadrant**

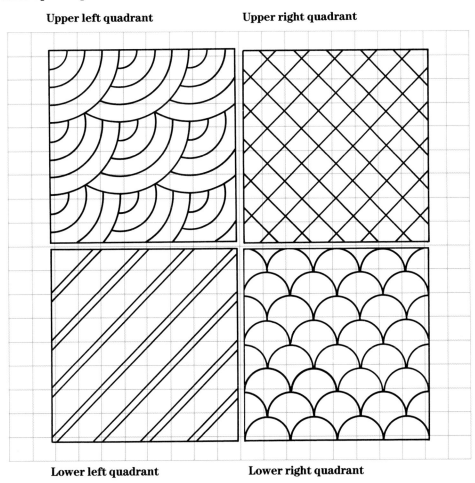

Lower left quadrant   **Lower right quadrant**

Figure 3. Overall pattern for Filler Pattern Sampler pillow

1. Fabric-Covered Cording. To make fabric-covered cording, you will need purchased cotton cable cord (which comes in a variety of widths and is available in most home-decorating departments) plus bias-cut strips of solid or print fabric. (For tips on preparing bias strips, see page 43.) Cut the strips of bias fabric 1 inch wider than the circumference of the cable cord. Stitch bias strips together on the diagonal to make the necessary yardage of bias binding.

With *wrong side* facing the cord, fold the fabric strip over the cord; pin and stitch. Use the zipper foot on your sewing machine and stitch close to the cording. Trim the fabric edges to within ¼ inch of stitching line.

With raw edges aligned and right sides facing, pin cording around the seam line of the pillow. Clip the seam allowance on the cording as you pin around the corners of the pillow; round the corners slightly so that the cording will lie flat against the fabric (see Figure 1). Stitch the cording to the pillow front (using the zipper foot) before assembling the pillow front and back. Then, with right sides facing, pin the pillow front and back together and again use the zipper foot to stitch the seam, with the foot pressed as close as possible to the cording for a neat finish.

Stitch around 3 sides and 4 corners; leave the bottom open for turning. Trim the corners and seams, turn the pillow right side out, press, stuff, and slip-stitch the fourth side closed.

2. *Ruffles.* As a general rule of thumb, fabric strips for ruffles should be cut twice the desired *width* of the ruffle (plus ½ inch for seam allowance), and 2 to 2½ times the measurement of the circumference of the pillow (plus ½ inch) in *length.*

For example, to make a 4-inch-wide ruffle for a 16-inch pillow top: Cut a strip of fabric 8½ inches wide by 128 to 160 inches long (pieced, if necessary, with seams pressed open). With right sides facing, sew the short ends of the strip together and press seam open. Fold the strip in half (wrong sides facing) and press.

By inserting pins along the raw edges of the ruffle, divide the length of the ruffle into fourths. Run a row of machine basting along the raw edges of each fourth of the strip, between the pins, so that each section of the ruffle can be gathered to fit one side of the pillow and adjusted separately.

Matching the raw edges of the ruffle and pillow top, gather, pin, and baste the ruffle to the right side of the pillow top (the folded edge of the ruffle will be facing in toward the center of the pillow).

Note: I find it easier to pin each quarter section of the ruffle from the center of one side to the center of the adjacent side, rather than from corner to corner. This makes it easier to adjust gathers evenly around each corner.

Stitch the ruffle to the pillow top and remove pins before pinning the back in place. Pin pillow back to front, and stitch the pillow together, stitching just *inside* the seam line joining the ruffle to the top. Stitch around 3 sides and 4 corners; leave the bottom open for turning. Trim the corners and seams, turn the pillow right side out, press, stuff, and slip-stitch the bottom closed.

3. *Combination Trim.* Always pin and stitch trim items to the pillow front in the order in which they appear on top of the pillow. If there is to be cording and a ruffle, for example, baste the cording to the pillow top first, then the ruffle. If there are 2 ruffles, a narrow and a wider one, stitch the inner ruffle of lace or fabric to the deeper ruffle first. Gather the layered ruffles as one unit, then pin and stitch the double ruffle to the pillow or quilt top with the inner (narrower) ruffle facing the pillow top.

Finishing Quilts and Coverlets
There are 3 basic ways to finish the raw edges of quilts, coverlets, and other patchwork pieces.

1. Bias Binding. Strips of bias-cut fabric, either narrow or wide, are often used to bind the edges of a quilt or wall hanging or to cover cotton cording for use as trim on pillows, quilts, and other projects. Packaged bias tape is available in fabric stores, but the color range is limited and you will want to make your own bias binding for most projects.

To cut bias strips, fold a square or rectangle of fabric in half on the diagonal and cut along the fold line (see Figure 2). Using a straight-edge ruler, measure, mark, and cut bias strips of the desired width parallel to this diagonal cut edge. To make longer strips, piece short bias strips on the diagonal, and press the seams open (see Figure 3).

To prepare bias strips for use as bindings, fold the raw edges of the long side of the strip in toward the center of the *wrong side* ¼ inch and press.

To attach bias binding to the edges of the quilt or other project, unfold one pressed edge of the bias strip and, with right sides facing, pin the strip along the edge of the quilt top. The creased foldline makes a convenient stitching line. Once the bias strip is stitched in place, fold the binding over to the back of the quilt and slip-stitch the folded edge along the seam line.

2. Self-Binding. A second way of finishing the edges of a quilt is the self-binding method. For this method, quilt backing must be at least 1 inch larger on each side than the batting and the quilt top. Trim batting to match quilt top and trim backing so that it extends exactly 1 inch beyond the edges of the quilt top on all sides. Then, with right side of the quilt facing up, fold the raw edges of the quilt backing under ¼ inch along all 4 sides and press. Fold the corners of the backing in over the quilt top and pin. Then fold the edges of the quilt backing onto the quilt front, neatly mitering the corners, and pin in place. Slip-stitch the self-binding in place as shown in Figure 4.

If the quilt top has a plain border, the border fabric can be used to bind the quilt edges. Just trim the backing and batting 1 inch smaller than the quilt top on all sides, and fold the edges of the border strips to the *back*, reversing the procedure described above.

3. Folded Edges. For a folded-edge finish, turn the raw edges of the backing fabric in over the batting ¼ to ½ inch and press. Then fold under the raw edges of the quilt top and slip-stitch the folded edges of the top and back together (see Figure 5).

Tips on Hanging Quilts and Other Patchwork
Note: Never, never, *never* put pushpins, tacks, or nails through a quilt, new or old. Eventually, the quilt will sag or tear from its own weight.

Two of the best methods to hang quilts are by stitching a simple muslin sleeve to the back of the quilt and inserting a curtain rod; or by basting the edges of the quilt to muslin strips stretched over a frame made from artist's stretchers.

1. Muslin Sleeve. The easiest way to mount a quilt that is to be hung on the

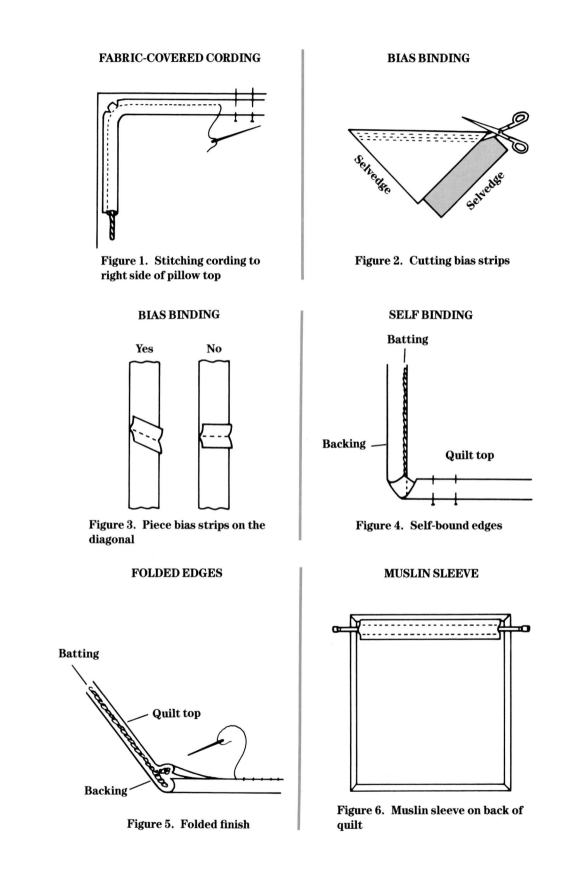

FABRIC-COVERED CORDING

Figure 1. Stitching cording to right side of pillow top

BIAS BINDING

Figure 2. Cutting bias strips

BIAS BINDING

Yes   No

Figure 3. Piece bias strips on the diagonal

SELF BINDING

Batting

Backing

Quilt top

Figure 4. Self-bound edges

FOLDED EDGES

Batting

Quilt top

Backing

Figure 5. Folded finish

MUSLIN SLEEVE

Figure 6. Muslin sleeve on back of quilt

44

square (that is, with top and bottom parallel to the floor) is on a rod slipped through a muslin sleeve that has been stitched to the back of the quilt. To make such a sleeve, cut a piece of muslin about 7 inches wide and as long as the top of the quilt, corner to corner. Stitch the long edges of the sleeve together to form a tube, press the seam open, and turn the sleeve right side out. Turn in the raw edges on each end of the tube and hem. Stitch this sleeve to the back of the quilted project as shown in Figure 6. Stitch just through the backing and into the batting but without penetrating the quilt top. Sew along the top and bottom of the sleeve, leaving enough play in the fabric so that a curtain rod can be slipped into the sleeve for hanging. Use one sleeve for small projects, several short sleeves spaced 6 to 10 inches apart for larger projects.

2. Stretchers. For quilts and small projects that are to be hung on the diagonal, hand stitch 6-inch-wide strips of muslin just inside the outer edges of the quilt or wall hanging. Fold the strips around a frame made of artist's stretchers (available in art supply stores) of an appropriate length and width. Pull the muslin to the back of the stretchers and staple. As with the muslin sleeves above, the muslin strips should be stitched to the quilt through its backing and into the batting, but not through the quilt top.

Tokens of Affection

One of the pleasures of patchwork is creating one-of-a-kind gifts for family and friends. In this section you'll find a potpourri of small gifts to make for everyone you love.

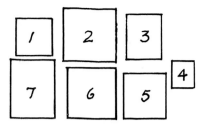

Patchwork picture mats. Frames 5 and 7: Monkey Wrench; frames 2 and 6: "found patchwork"; frames 1 and 3: lace and ribbon; frame 4: lace doily

Patchwork Picture Mats

Favorite photographs and treasured memorabilia deserve a fitting display, and these fabric-covered mats — some of true patchwork and some of the cut-and-paste variety — are a clever way to turn thrift shop finds into personalized frames.

Try some of the following ideas to duplicate the frames shown on the preceding pages. Make just one or two as gifts, or create a whole patchwork gallery for a stairway or hall.

General Materials List

scraps of assorted fabrics and/or pieces of old pieced or appliquéd patchwork squares.
squares and rectangles of lightweight cardboard for backing patchwork mats
purchased or recycled picture frames
white craft glue, glue stick, and/or spray adhesive
masking tape or packing tape
scissors and compass
narrow piping, decorative trim, and/or grosgrain ribbon for edging mat openings
strips of lace and/or ribbon
mat knife
cardboard or plastic for templates

General Directions

1. Cut a square or rectangle of cardboard slightly smaller than the inside back opening of a purchased frame (to allow for fabric bulk).

2. Trace and cut a square, rectangle, circle or oval from the center of the cardboard, using a mat knife or scissors. Make sure the opening is a suitable size for the picture you plan to frame.

3. Cut a piece of fabric (or pieced patchwork) at least ½ inch larger on all sides than the cardboard mat.

4. Center and glue fabric on one side of the mat. Cut the center from the fabric, leaving at least ½-inch seam allowance. Clip the curves and corners, fold the fabric through the center opening to the back of the cardboard and glue in place. Fold the raw edges on the top, bottom, and sides of the mat to the back and secure with dabs of glue or strips of packing tape, as shown in Figure 1.

5. Embellish the basic fabric-covered mat as shown in the photo and described in the specific directions that follow.

Tape   Glue clipped edges

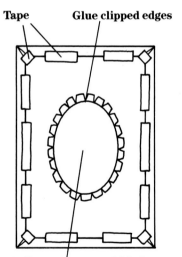

Cut out center of fabric

Figure 1. Back of fabric-covered mat

48

Tips for Perfect Picture Mats

1. Work with lightweight, non-bulky fabrics and trims to avoid making mats that are too thick to fit into the frame.

2. Make sure that the fabric is tacked securely to the cardboard backing, so that it won't slip or sag in the frame. Don't overdo the glue, however; it may seep through and stain the fabric and trim.

3. Keep the photo or memento you plan to frame handy as you design the mat, to make sure the colors, scale, and pattern of the mat design complement rather than overwhelm the picture.

4. Most mats will look more finished with a second, inner mat or a row of trim glued around the inside opening. Refer to the photo for ideas.

PIECED PATCHWORK MATS

Some pieced patchwork block designs are perfect for mat frames, especially those with a center square that can be enlarged or reduced easily to accommodate the desired size opening. The familiar Monkey Wrench pattern (adapted for frames 5 and 7) is one such block. Pieced as a 10-inch square with a 4½-inch opening, it provides a nice wide mat for a square picture (frame 5). By simply lengthening the side strips of the block, the same pattern stretches to fill a

Each square equals 1 inch

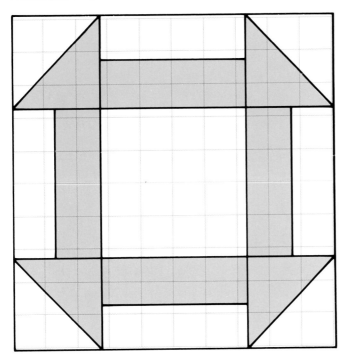

Figure 2. Assembly diagram for Monkey Wrench block

10 × 13-inch frame (frame 7). By varying the length and width of the side strips on the pattern block, you can adjust the pattern to any size frame.

Refer to Figure 2 for the pattern and assembly diagram for a 10-inch Monkey Wrench mat.

To Piece the Monkey Wrench Mat:

1. Enlarge the pattern on page 49 to desired size and cut out templates for the triangle, square, and rectangular strips. Add ½-inch seam allowances to each piece.

2. Cut and piece the pattern block from fabric scraps. Press the completed block.

3. Cut a cardboard mat with the outside dimensions of the finished patchwork block (10 × 10 inches) and with a center opening slightly smaller than the center square of the block (about 4 × 4 inches).

4. Center and tack the pieced block to the cardboard mat with *light* dabs of glue. (Use a glue stick or a light coating of spray adhesive rather than liquid glue.) Cut out center square, leaving a ½- to ¾-inch seam allowance. Clip seam allowance and fold the fabric to the back of the frame and glue or tape in place. Turn the raw edges of the block to the back on top, bottom, and sides; glue or tape fabric edges to back of cardboard mat.

5. Edge the center opening with strips of grosgrain ribbon or other trim to give the mat a more finished look. Glue edging in place. Position picture or memento on back of mat, tape in place, and slip into the frame.

6. Instead of piecing your own mats, you might look for scrap blocks of patchwork at yard sales or fabric shops. (Such "found patchwork" was used for frames 2 and 6.) Note that it is not necessary for the center opening to correspond exactly to the patchwork pattern. A circular opening can be cut from the center of a square block, for example.

LACE AND RIBBON PATCHWORK MATS

Pretty effects can also be achieved by trimming a plain fabric-covered mat with stitched or glued-on lattice designs of ribbon and/or bands of lace trim (see frames 1 and 3). To avoid bulk, the ribbon and lace can be trimmed and glued at the edge of the mat, rather than folded to the back.

LACE DOILY PICTURE MAT

To make an especially romantic mat for a very special picture, stitch or glue an old lace doily, with the fabric center removed and the inside edges trimmed or hemmed, to a fabric-covered mat. For the background fabric, choose a color that will display the lace to the best advantage (see Frame 4).

Appliquéd Guest Towels

Victorian ladies appliquéd entire quilts with wreaths and garlands of flowers cut from chintz; you can use the same technique (called *Broderie Perse*) to embellish smaller items as well, like the dainty guest towels pictured on page 52.

Start with purchased hand towels or make your own (count on making three 13 × 17½-inch towels from a half yard of 45-inch linen or huck toweling). Use scraps of any pretty floral print for the appliqués. If the intricate shapes of flowers and leaves tax your appliqué skills, just cut out heart shapes and stitch them instead. Trim each towel with a dash of ribbon and/or lace if you like — but make sure that all materials are washable and preshrunk.

Materials
purchased hand towels or one 13½ × 18-inch rectangle of fabric for each towel
scraps of floral print cotton chintz
13½-inch strips of preshrunk ribbon and/or lace for trim (optional)

Directions

1. If you're making your towels from scratch, cut a 13½ × 18-inch rectangle of fabric for each towel. Make a ¼-inch hem on the top and sides. Leave the bottom unhemmed if you plan to add lace trim; otherwise hem the bottom edge as well.

2. Snip a selection of flowers and leaves or other motifs from chintz fabric. Leave a ⅛-inch seam allowance around each motif for machine appliqué, or a ¼-inch seam allowance for hand appliqué.

3. Position a heart patch or a few flowers and leaves on the bottom of each towel, 2 to 3 inches up from the bottom edge. Baste, pin, or tack the shapes in place with fabric glue.

4. Appliqué shapes to the towel by hand or machine (see page 27 for appliqué stitching details).

5. Trim each towel with rows of ribbon and/or an edging of lace, if desired. Refer to the photo for suggestions. Topstitch ribbon and lace trim in place.

Broderie Perse appliqué is a lovely way to embellish all sorts of purchased items, such as place mats and napkins, apron pockets, and pillow tops. Keep an eye out for pretty fabric remnants with well-defined motifs that can be used for *Broderie Perse* projects; your supply will come in handy for trimming purchased linens and the like for last-minute gifts.

Crazy Quilt Projects

In piecing one of these projects for a special friend, you might include a sentimental patch or two in the design: a scrap from her first quilting project or favorite dress, a bit of antique embroidery, a souvenir ribbon, or some other fabric memento. Or just tuck a little heart-shaped patch in among the crazy pieces.

CRAZY QUILT SEWING ACCESSORIES

Stitched from the scraps of patchwork projects past, these crazy quilt accessories make splendid gifts for anyone who likes to sew. The eyeglass case, needle book, and pincushion are all pieced from scraps of wool, satin, and velveteen in rich, dark colors. You might prefer a pastel palette (see the crazy patch pillow on page 33 as an example) or a selection of more traditional calico prints and solids. Use whatever fabrics you have on hand, or any mix that suits your fancy.

Because these articles are small, I used only a bit of featherstitching along the seams between crazy patches, but you can certainly use more (or less) elaborate embroidery if you like.

Materials
scraps of light- to medium-weight fabrics in desired range of colors
½ yard lightweight muslin for background fabric
½ yard satiny fabric for lining
cardboard or plastic for templates

for eyeglass case:
    1 yard contrasting bias binding
    12 × 12-inch scrap of lightweight batting
    1 ornamental button for closure

for needle book:
    scraps of closely woven flannel for leaves of book
    ½ yard contrasting bias binding
    scraps of cardboard
    ½ yard satin ribbon

for pincushion:
    ⅔ yard fabric-covered cording
    scrap of wool fabric for backing
    fiber fill

Directions

Note: Patterns and yardage measurements throughout include ½-inch seam allowances, instead of the usual ¼-inch allowance, because the muslin background piece is likely to "shrink" slightly as crazy quilt patches are applied.

EYEGLASS CASE

1. Enlarge patterns for the front and back of the case (page 56) to the desired size. Add ½-inch seam allowances to each piece and cut templates. For each piece, trace and cut one shape from muslin; cut matching pieces from light-weight batting and from lining fabric. Set the batting and lining shapes aside.

2. Arrange scraps of fabric in a pleasing design on muslin pattern pieces. Fabric patches should extend a little beyond the raw edges of the muslin. Stitch crazy quilt patches in place by hand or machine, as detailed on pages 32–34.

3. Baste around the edges of the front and back shapes; trim the excess patch fabric back to match the muslin pieces.

4. Embellish seams with featherstitching or other embroidery if you like. See page 36 for embroidery stitch illustrations.

5. Slip matching piece of batting between pieced front and lining fabric and baste through all 3 layers ⅛-inch in from raw edge. Repeat for the back of the case. Trim the excess fabric as necessary.

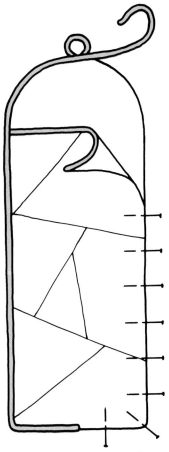

**Figure 1. Cover edges of case
with bias binding**

6. Cover the top of the case front with a narrow strip of bias binding cut from a contrasting fabric (or from lining fabric). See Figure 1. With lining sides facing, pin the case front and back together and cover the raw edges with bias binding, stitching up one side, around flap, down second side, and across bottom. See page 43 for details on bias binding.

7. Before tacking down the binding at the center of the flap, insert and stitch in place a small loop of bias binding or cording for the button closure. Stitch binding in place. Position the button on the case front and sew in place.

Each square equals 1 inch

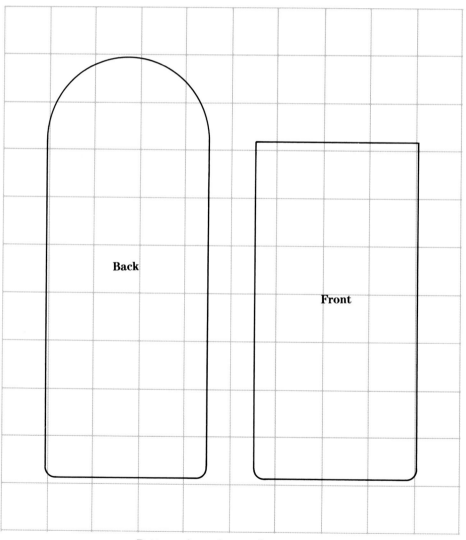

Pattern pieces for eyeglass case

NEEDLE BOOK

My grandmother kept a needle book like this one in her sewing box — a legacy from days when a fine, sharp needle was a treasured tool, to be carefully husbanded. Good needles are now available everywhere for a song, but, thanks to my grandmother, I've always considered a needle book an essential part of a well-stocked sewing kit. If you're less sentimental, you might adapt the pattern to make a card case or stamp book as a stocking-stuffer gift. Instructions for these are included following the needle book instructions.

1. Cut a 4¼ × 6½-inch rectangle of muslin and a matching piece of lining fabric. Set the lining aside.

2. Piece and stitch a crazy patch design on the muslin background fabric and embellish the seams between patches with featherstitching or other embroidery (see page 36 for stitch illustrations). Trim raw edges.

3. With *wrong* sides facing, pin and baste the satin lining to the pieced front of the case. Baste around 3 sides (¼-inch seams), leaving bottom open.

4. With light pencil strokes, mark a line down the center of the lining as a guide, then machine stitch parallel seams ⅛-inch on either side of that line, making 2 pockets.

5. Cut 2 rectangles of cardboard just large enough to slip into each pocket of the case (see Figure 2). Slip one piece of cardboard into each pocket; baste closed the seam allowance along the bottom of the case.

6. Use pinking shears to cut 2 or 3 rectangles of thin, closely woven flannel or other tightly woven fabric for the book's leaves. Rectangles should measure approximately 3¼ × 6 inches. Layer the leaves together and topstitch them to the center of the needle book (see Figure 3).

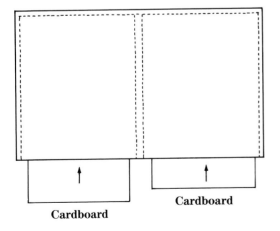

Cardboard

Cardboard

Figure 2. Slip cardboards into pockets of book

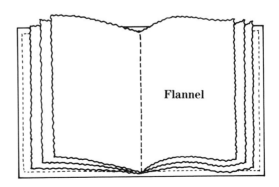

Flannel

Figure 3. Stitch flannel leaves in needle book

7. Appliqué a length of ribbon or contrasting bias fabric along the spine of the book to conceal the seams. Bind the edges of the book with bias strips, as for the eyeglass case (see Figure 1, page 55).

8. Stitch one end of a 6-inch length of narrow satin ribbon to the center edge of the front cover; stitch a matching piece to the back cover of the book for ties.

CARD CASE OR STAMP BOOK

Adjust the needle book design to fit business cards or stamp books. After stitching lining fabric to the pieced top (see step 3, above), cut and hem two rectangles of lining fabric and baste one to each half of the book to make pockets for cards or stamp books (see Figure 4). Eliminate the leaves meant to hold needles and finish the case with a button and loop closure, rather than ribbon ties.

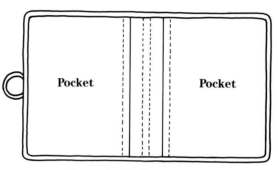

Figure 4. Card or stamp case

PINCUSHION

I happen to like a fair-size pincushion that can accommodate lots of pins without seeming "prickly," so this one measures a generous 7 inches square — but of course you can make one any size (or shape) you prefer.

1. Cut an 8-inch square of muslin and a matching square of backing fabric.

2. Appliqué the square in a crazy quilt pattern as detailed in instructions for making the eyeglass case. Embroider seams as desired (see page 36 for embroidery illustrations).

3. Trim the fabric patches to match the edges of the muslin square. Baste around all 4 edges. Add fabric-covered cording if desired (see page 41 for cording details).

4. With right sides facing, pin the square of backing fabric to the pieced front. Stitch around 3 sides and 4 corners. Trim the corners and seams.

5. Turn the pincushion right side out, press, stuff with fiber fill, and slip-stitch the opening closed. I've added a loop of ribbon to one corner to hang the pincushion on the wall near my worktable, but this detail is optional.

PATCHWORK DISPLAY PILLOW

A friend of mine who doesn't quilt, but who cherishes every piece of handwork that comes her way, has been wonderfully inventive about finding ways to display her stitchery treasures. For instance, she puts this antique crazy quilt heart to work as a dresser-top display pillow for a special collection of pins and brooches.

To make a similar display piece for your own collectibles, cut a heart-shaped piece of muslin of the desired dimensions (this one measures about 12×12 inches). Also cut matching shapes of batting and backing. Appliqué the muslin heart with crazy patches and embroider as desired (see page 36 for embroidery illustrations). Baste the top, batting, and backing together and bind the edges with contrasting strips of bias fabric.

Stitched from calico prints and other washable fabrics, this pieced heart design would also make a delightful hot pad or decorative table mat.

Gifts From Bow Tie Blocks

The jaunty Bow Tie block (also known as True Lover's Knot) lends itself to any number of single- and multiple-block projects. Make up batches of 3-inch Bow Tie squares from assorted fabrics whenever you have the time, then piece the patches into small gifts as the need arises. Make enough blocks, of course, and there's a quilt in the offing — but sometimes the smaller projects are more fun to make (and certainly faster to finish!).

BASIC BOW TIE BLOCK

Materials

scraps of printed, striped, or plaid fabric for Bow Ties
scraps of contrasting fabrics (light or dark) for the background of each block
cardboard or plastic for templates

Directions

1. Trace and cut templates for pattern pieces (*A*) and (*B*). Patterns include ¼-inch seam allowances.

2. Trace templates onto *wrong side* of fabrics and cut the following pieces for each block:
   (*A*) 1 from Bow Tie fabric
   (*B*) 2 from Bow Tie fabric
       2 from background fabric

3. Assemble the block, referring to Figure 1 (first, piece the tie portion of the block, then add the background piece to complete the remaining corners of the square). Press seams toward the tie.

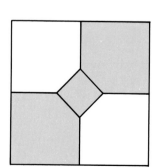
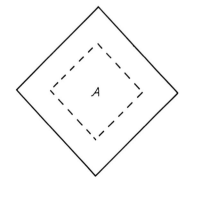
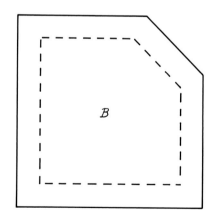

Figure 1. Assembly diagram

Pattern pieces for Bow Tie block

60

BOW TIE BLOCK SACHETS

Make the pillow sachets shown below of shirting fabrics and fill with cedar chips or a moth-deterring mixture of lavender, rosemary, and orris root, then tuck them among blankets and sweaters. Stitched in pastel prints and filled with lavender, dried rose petals, or your favorite blend of scented herbs and spices, they make sweet-smelling sachets for lingerie and linen drawers. (Potpourris, sachet powders, and other scented mixtures are available by mail order from a number of reputable sources; or check your Yellow Pages for local suppliers.)

1. Make one Bow Tie block from desired fabrics, as detailed in the general directions on the facing page.

2. Border the 3-inch block with 1-inch-wide strips of contrasting fabric (use ¼-inch seams).

3. Pin and stitch decorative cording or narrow ruffles of fabric or eyelet lace around the edges of the pieced block, if desired (see pages 41–42 for details on ruffles and cording).

4. Cut, pin, and stitch a matching square of backing fabric to the pieced top, stitching around 3 sides and 4 corners. Trim corners, turn, and press.

5. Stuff the pillow loosely with a mixture of fiber fill and sachet powder or other scented mixture, as described above. Slip-stitch the fourth side closed.

BOW TIE BOXES

1. Purchase a wooden craft box with a recessed lid (available at local craft and needlework shops). The smaller box pictured on page 61 has a 5×5-inch insert space; the larger box has room for an 8×8-inch insert.

2. For the smaller box: Piece one 3×3-inch Bow Tie square from your favorite fabrics and frame the square with 1½-inch-wide strips of contrasting fabric (¼-inch seams).

   For the larger box: Make 4 Bow Tie squares and piece them together to form a larger block, as shown in photo. Edge the block with 1½-inch-wide strips of contrasting fabric (¼-inch seams). Press seams.

3. Layer the pieced Bow Tie square together with matching squares of batting and muslin backing; baste. Quilt the square as desired.

4. Remove the square of cardboard backing from the box lid. Center the quilted Bow Tie block on the backing and secure the cardboard with dabs of craft glue. Insert backing (Bow Tie side up) into the box lid and secure with small nails.

BOW TIE POTHOLDERS

1. Make 4 matching (or different) Bow Tie squares from washable fabrics, as described on page 60.

2. Pin and stitch the 4 blocks together (refer to the photo on the facing page for possible block arrangements). Press seams.

3. Border the pieced potholder with 1-inch-wide strips of contrasting fabric (¼-inch seams).

4. Cut a matching piece of backing fabric and a *double* layer of polyester fleece or a thick slab of batting. Baste batting, backing, and the pieced Bow Tie block together. Outline quilt the Bow Tie shapes, if desired, or quilt along seams.

5. Bind the raw edges of the potholder with matching or contrasting bias tape and add a loop of bias tape or cording at one corner for hanging.

APPLIQUÉD TEA TOWELS

1. Piece 3 or 4 Bow Ties (just the tie portion, not the entire block). Press under the seam allowances on each tie.

2. Appliqué the ties in a row across the bottom of a purchased linen tea towel. Refer to the photo for positioning.

Gifts of the Heart

Following are 3 heart-pattern projects for special-occasion gifts: a pieced and appliquéd wedding square, a classic crib quilt, and a lace appliqué hanging that you can make in an afternoon.

PATCHWORK HEART WEDDING PIECE

Stitched from a traditional mix of shirting fabrics (his) and dainty prints (hers), the medallion design pictured on the next page is adapted from the center panel of an early nineteenth-century wedding quilt made in New Jersey. You may want to embroider or quilt a special date or message in the center heart or along the border strips to personalize the piece. The finished piece measures 28×28 inches.

Materials

1 yard assorted gingham and shirting scraps for triangles
⅜ yard muslin for squares
⅜ yard assorted small prints for hearts
scrap of red cotton for center heart
⅓ yard contrasting fabric for borders
28×28-inch square of light- or medium-weight batting
28×28-inch square of backing fabric
cardboard or plastic for templates

Directions

1. Trace full-size patterns (page 66) and make separate templates for square (*A*), triangle (*B*), and heart (*C*). Add ¼-inch seam allowances to each piece.

2. Trace and cut the following pieces:
   (*A*) 9 muslin squares
   (*B*) 28 triangles, cut from assorted light and dark gingham and shirting fabrics
       8 blue triangles for center star design
   (*C*) 8 hearts from print fabric
       1 heart from solid red fabric

3. Appliqué 1 heart to the center of each muslin square (see page 26 for appliqué details). On the original New Jersey quilt, each heart was appliquéd with buttonhole stitching, but we've used plain whipstitching here.

4. Use pencil or fabric marker to trace a date or message on the center of the red heart if desired. Embroider the message in outline stitch (see page 36).

5. Arrange squares and triangles to form 3 rows of 3 blocks each, taking care that the placement of the blue triangles produces the star pattern shown in Figure 1.

6. Pin and stitch each individual block; press. Assemble the pieced blocks to form each row, then stitch the 3 rows together to complete the pieced top. Match all corners and seams very carefully.

7. Cut 2 strips of border fabric, each 3 × 24½ inches. Cut 2 more strips, each 3 × 30 inches. Pin and stitch shorter strips to 2 opposite sides of the pieced square. Press seam toward borders. Pin and stitch longer strips to the top and bottom of the square; press seams toward borders.

To Complete the Wall Hanging

1. Cut batting and backing 1 inch smaller all around than pieced top. Center and baste the batting, backing, and pieced top together as detailed on page 38.

2. Turn raw edges of border strips under ¼ inch, fold to the back of the quilt, and slip-stitch in place. Refer to page 43 for details on self-binding.

3. Quilt the wall hanging as desired (I outline-quilted around each heart and along all seam lines).

4. See page 45 for tips on how to mount the finished piece.

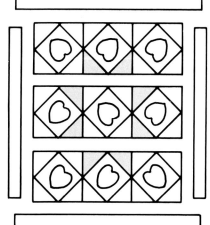

Figure 1. Assembly diagram for Wedding Piece

Pattern pieces for Wedding Piece

B

C

A

66

SWEET HEART CRIB QUILT

Use repeats of the 6-inch appliquéd heart squares picked up from the Wedding Piece pattern on the facing page to create this crib quilt for a very special baby. Choose all pink or all blue hearts if you're a traditionalist, or mix and match hearts in all colors of the rainbow, as I did here. If you piece and quilt the squares by machine, you can easily finish this 40 × 46-inch coverlet in a weekend.

Materials

3 yards muslin for blocks and backing
40 × 46-inch rectangle of batting
6-inch squares of 42 different print fabrics for heart appliqués
⅓ yard contrasting fabric for borders
cardboard or plastic for templates

Directions

1. Trace the heart pattern (*C*) on page 66 and cut a cardboard or plastic template. Do *not* add seam allowance.

2. Trace the outline of the heart on the *right* side of each square of print fabric.

   Hint: Before cutting out the appliqué shapes, machine stitch along the traced outline, then cut out each heart, leaving a ¼-inch seam allowance for hand appliqué and a scant ¹⁄₁₆ inch beyond the stitched line for machine appliqué. This machine-stitched outline will help each heart hold its shape as you appliqué the motif in place.

3. Cut 42 muslin squares, each 6½ × 6½ inches, and appliqué 1 heart to the center of each square by hand or machine.

4. Arrange the appliquéd squares in 7 horizontal rows of 6 blocks each. Piece the blocks together to make 7 strips (¼-inch seams); piece the strips together to complete the quilt top.

5. Cut four 3 × 44-inch strips of fabric for borders. Stitch 1 border strip to each side of the quilt first, and then stitch strips to the top and bottom, trimming the length of each strip as necessary.

6. Cut rectangles of muslin and batting 1 inch smaller on all sides than the pieced top. Center, pin, and baste appliquéd top, batting, and backing together.

7. Quilt the coverlet as desired. You can either outline quilt around each heart and along the seam lines, quilt "in the ditch," or simply tie the quilt at the corners of each pattern block. See pages 37–40 for details on quilting.

8. Turn the raw edges of the border under, miter corners, fold borders to the back, and slip-stitch edges to the backing. (See page 43 for details on self-binding.)

LACE HEART WALL HANGING

The patterned lace wall hanging, opposite, is a breeze to stitch from purchased lace and pieced or printed background fabric. Patterned lace is available in a wide variety of patterns—birds, houses, cherubs, and flowers, as well as the lovely design of 6-inch heart blocks used for this hanging. To enliven the white-on-white motifs, I lined and framed a 30-inch square of lace with pieces cut from an old pieced quilt top that had seen better days. The stains and worn spots on the quilt top don't show through the lace, but the color comes through beautifully. A brightly patterned piece of print fabric — the bolder and brighter the better — would work just as well for the backing.

To make a similar wall hanging, machine-stitch a 30½ × 30½-inch panel of purchased lace on top of a matching square of background fabric. From the same background/lining fabric, cut 2 border strips, each 3½ × 30½ inches, for the sides, and 2 strips, each 3½ × 36½ inches, for the top and bottom borders. Pin and stitch the borders in place.

Next, layer and baste the lined lace design together with a piece of batting and a square of muslin backing fabric. Quilt in the seam around the inside edge of the frame. Bind the raw edges of the hanging with contrasting bias tape and add a sleeve of muslin along the top back of the square for hanging. For instructions on hanging, refer to page 44.

Cottage Patchwork: Designs for the Home

You don't need to tackle a quilt-size project to introduce patchwork into your home decorating scheme. Here are pieced and appliquéd projects to enliven every room in the house — from an appliquéd tea cozy to quilted wall hangings.

APPLIQUÉD TEA COZY

This patchwork cozy keeps the tea hot and the kitchen cheery — and it's yours to decorate as fancy dictates. Use the basic pattern and the color photo for inspiration, then trim the house and "landscape" the grounds as you like.

Materials

½ yard *each* sky-blue fabric for the cozy and calico for the lining
scraps of green cotton for grass, tree, and bushes
scraps of yellow, red, and blue fabric for house
scraps of lace, ribbon, decorative braid, and buttons for trim
1 yard fabric-covered cording for edging
thick polyester fleece for backing
paper or cardboard for templates

Directions

Note: These patterns do not include seam allowances. Add ¼-inch seam allowances where indicated. Finished cozy is 11 × 15 inches.

1. Enlarge the pattern to size and cut templates for the cozy and the basic appliqué shapes. Templates do not include seam allowances.

2. Trace and cut 2 curved tea cozy shapes from blue fabric and cut matching shapes from fleece and from fabric (add ¼-inch seam allowances to all pieces).

3. Trace and cut appliqué shapes from desired fabrics (add ¼-inch seam allowances to each piece for hand appliqué; omit seam allowances for machine appliqué).

4. Lay a band of grass green fabric (about 2 inches wide) across the bottom of the blue cozy front. Now "build" your house on this background landscape, working from background pieces toward foreground to achieve the desired design.

   First, cut the window rectangles out of the house shape, baste under seam allowance, and position the house on the grass. Position the door on the house front. Tuck scraps of lace trim inside the window openings for curtains. Add the roof and chimney. Slip a billow of smoke (cut from opaque lace fabric) atop the chimney. Arrange all pieces before pinning and basting the entire scene in place.

5. Appliqué shapes by hand or machine (see page 26 for appliqué details). Add further embellishments as desired, such as a small button for the door knob, ribbon window boxes, flower print bushes, and so forth.

To Complete the Cozy

1. Baste a layer of polyester fleece to the back and front pieces of the cozy. Quilt the roof and other details of the appliquéd picture as desired. Refer to the photo on pages 70–71 for suggestions.

2. Pin and stitch fabric-covered cording around the curved top of the cozy front, adding a small loop at the center top for lifting the cover.

3. With right sides facing, pin and stitch back to front around the curved edges, leaving the bottom open. Clip curves, trim seam, turn, and press. Turn under bottom edges and press.

4. With right sides facing, stitch back and front linings together along the curved seam. Turn under the raw edges along the bottom, slip the lining inside the cozy and slip-stitch the lining to the appliquéd cover around the bottom edge. Also tack the lining to the cozy cover at several points along the inside seam.

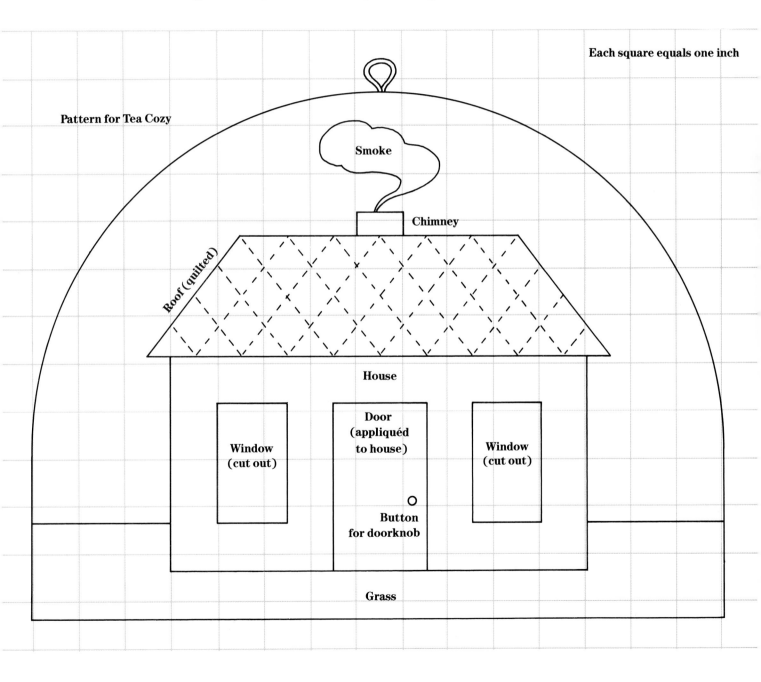

Each square equals one inch

Pattern for Tea Cozy

Smoke

Chimney

Roof (quilted)

House

Window (cut out)

Door (appliquéd to house)

Window (cut out)

Button for doorknob

Grass

Fan Pattern Projects

These fanciful designs (forgive the pun) are a great way to make use of even your tiniest scraps of pretty print fabrics. The more varied the spokes from fan to fan, the livelier the overall pattern will be.

Each project — the place mat set, companion hot pad, and handsome wall hanging — illustrates a different arrangement of the basic fan block, offering an opportunity to experiment with a variety of fan block designs before tackling a major quilt-size project (like the Wanderer pattern on page 132).

You will note that the fan block is pieced on a curve — a technique that's somewhat difficult to master if you haven't tried it before, but one that becomes easier with practice. Note that the larger projects pictured here (the place mats and wall hanging) are what I call "forgiving" designs. This simply means that, even if the individual fan blocks are not pieced to perfection, the overall set of the blocks will look fine as long as the outside seam lines on each completed square are marked and matched with care. The intention here is not to encourage sloppy piecing, but merely to discourage waste. When learning a new technique or practicing an old one, I often find it takes several tries to get it right, and I like to be able to put these practice squares to use in a project, rather than just tossing them out.

On the other hand, when you come to the hot pad design, you'll discover that this particular block arrangement doesn't really work unless the squares that make up the 4-block pattern are very carefully pieced so that the spokes of the 4 fans meet to form a perfect circle.

Directions begin below with basic information for piecing a single fan block. Details for each of the fan block projects follow.

SINGLE FAN BLOCK

Materials

scraps of solid lilac and solid white, plus scraps of 5 different print fabrics
clear plastic for templates

Directions

Note: Patterns include ¼-inch seam allowances.

1. Trace pattern pieces (page 81) and transfer to clear plastic to make templates.

2. For *each* fan square, cut the following (mark and cut all notches and mark seam lines carefully):

   (*A*) 1 lilac
   (*B*) 5 pieces, each from a different print fabric
   (*C*) 1 white

3. To begin, pin and stitch the 5 (*B*) fan spokes together to form the arc of the fan, as shown in Figure 1. Press seams to one side.

4. Piece the lilac base of the fan (*A*) to the fan spokes, carefully matching the notches on piece (*A*) to the seams between spokes on the arc of the fan. Press the seam toward the base of the fan.

5. Pin and stitch the completed fan to the white background shape — piece (*C*) — matching the seams between the spokes on the arc of the fan to the notches on piece (*C*). Press the seam toward the base of the fan.

6. It is important to accurately mark the stitching lines on each pieced fan block before assembling squares into larger pattern blocks. To mark seam lines, first cut a 5-inch square of clear plastic. Make a notch on each of 2 adjacent sides at exactly 2 inches and again at 4 inches up from one corner of the square, as shown in Figure 2. Center this notched plastic square on the *wrong* side of a pieced fan block and adjust so that the notches fall as nearly as possible at the seam lines between (*A*) and (*B*) and between (*B*) and (*C*). Now, using a pencil or fabric marker, trace around the 5-inch square onto the back of the pieced fan square. Use these traced lines as stitching lines when joining blocks together. Repeat for each block.

7. Piece and mark as many fan blocks as required for a specific project.

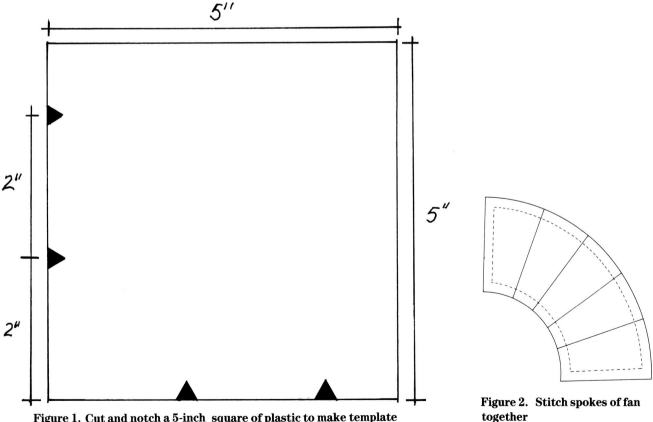

Figure 1. Cut and notch a 5-inch square of plastic to make template for marking seams

Figure 2. Stitch spokes of fan together

PRETTY PLACE MATS

Instructions are for two 13 × 19-inch mats

Materials

¾ yard white fabric for background and backing
⅛ yard lilac fabric
scraps of floral print fabrics in assorted colors and patterns
¼ yard red fabric for borders
two 14 × 20-inch rectangles of medium-weight batting
3⅔ yards lilac bias binding
clear plastic for templates

Directions

Note: All patterns and measurements include ¼-inch seam allowances.

1. Complete 6 fan blocks (as described on pages 74–75) for *each* place mat.

2. Cut 3 strips of red fabric, each 1½ × 5½ inches. Pin and stitch 1 strip between 2 fan squares, as shown in Figure 3. Repeat for 2 more pairs of fan squares. Press seams toward the red fabric.

3. Cut 4 strips of red fabric, each 1½ × 11½ inches. Pin and stitch 1 strip between 2 pairs of fan blocks. Add a second strip and a third pair of fan blocks. Pin and stitch remaining 2 strips to either end of the pieced blocks. Press seams toward the red strips.

4. For the top and bottom of each place mat, cut two 1½ × 19½-inch strips of red fabric. Pin and stitch border strips to the top and bottom of the mat. Press the seams toward borders.

Figure 3. Assembly diagram for place mats

To Assemble the Place Mat:

1. Cut batting and backing fabrics to size. Layer backing, batting, and the pieced top together; pin and baste through all 3 layers.

2. Machine or hand quilt "in the ditch" along seam lines between the sashing strips and the pieced blocks. (See page 37 for quilting details.) Remove basting.

3. Bind raw edges of each mat with lilac bias binding; slip-stitch binding to the wrong side of the mat.

FALLING TIMBERS WALL HANGING

Pieced in a pattern called Falling Timbers or Friendship Chain, this vibrant wall hanging measures 36×41 inches (a good size for a crib quilt). It's composed of 42 fan blocks arranged in 6 rows of 7 squares each, bordered with 3-inch-wide strips of red print fabric and finished with a narrow band of lilac bias binding. Note that the white fabric used for background piece (C) varies a shade or two from square to square, which adds, I think, an interesting texture to the pattern.

Materials

(A) ¼ yard lilac fabric
(B) approximately 1 yard mixed floral print scraps
(C and backing) 2 yards white fabric
½ yard red print fabric for borders
5 yards lilac bias binding
medium-weight batting
clear plastic for templates

Directions

Note: All patterns and measurements include ¼-inch seam allowances.

1. Cut and piece 42 fan squares as described in the basic instructions on pages 74–75. Mark the seam lines on each block.

2. Arrange the 42 blocks in 6 rows of 7 squares each, alternating block arrangements between Row A and Row B, as shown in Figure 4. Lay out 3 of Row A and 3 of Row B.

3. Pin and stitch the squares in each row together; press the seams open. Then pin and stitch the 6 rows together, alternating A and B rows and carefully matching seams. Press the seams open.

4. Cut 2 strips of red fabric, each $3\frac{1}{2} \times 35$ inches. Pin and stitch these border strips to the top and bottom of the pieced top. Then cut 2 strips of red fabric, each $3\frac{1}{2} \times 36\frac{1}{2}$ inches. Pin and stitch 1 strip to each side of the quilt top. Press the seams toward borders.

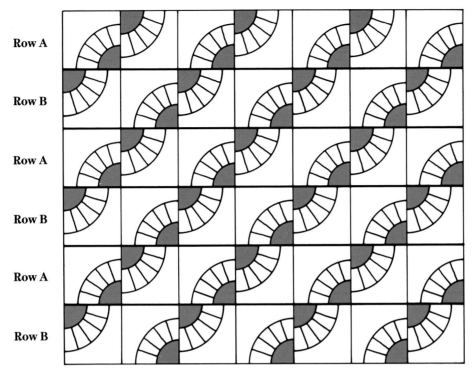

Row A

Row B

Row A

Row B

Row A

Row B

Figure 4. Assembly diagram for Falling Timbers wall hanging

To Finish the Wall Hanging

1. Cut backing and batting to size. Pin and baste backing, batting, and the pieced top together.
2. Hand quilt ¼ inch beyond the seam lines, outlining each fan shape (see page 38 for quilting details).
3. Trim and bind raw edges of the quilt with narrow strips of lilac bias binding.
4. To hang: Hand stitch a 1½-inch-wide sleeve of backing fabric along the top edge of the quilt and insert a narrow curtain rod for hanging (see page 44 for details of hanging a quilt).

TARGET PATTERN HOT PAD

Materials

(A) ⅛ yard lilac fabric
(B) ⅛ yard *each* assorted floral print fabrics
(C and backing) ½ yard white fabric
⅛ yard red print fabric for borders
1½ yards lilac bias binding (1½ inches wide)
clear plastic for templates
14-inch square of thick polyester fleece

Directions

Note: All patterns and measurements include ¼-inch seam allowances.

1. Cut and piece 4 fan squares and mark 5-inch-square seam allowances, using a checking template as described and shown on page 75.

2. Pin and stitch the squares in 2 rows of 2 squares each, as shown in Figure 5, taking special care to match the seams where the fans meet at each edge.

3. Pin and stitch the 2 halves of the circular design together, again matching seams carefully.

4. Cut four 1½-inch-wide strips of red print fabric and stitch 1 to the top and 1 to the bottom, then 1 to each side of the hot pad square. Press the seams toward borders.

5. Center and baste the pieced top on 14-inch squares of polyester fleece and backing. Machine quilt around the circled seams and around the inside of the red borders.

6. Pin and stitch lilac bias binding around the red border strips of the hot pad, as described for place mats on page 77.

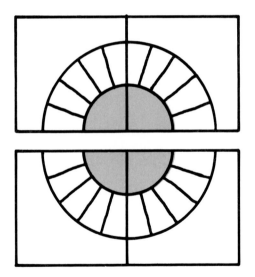

Figure 5. Assembly diagram for hot pad

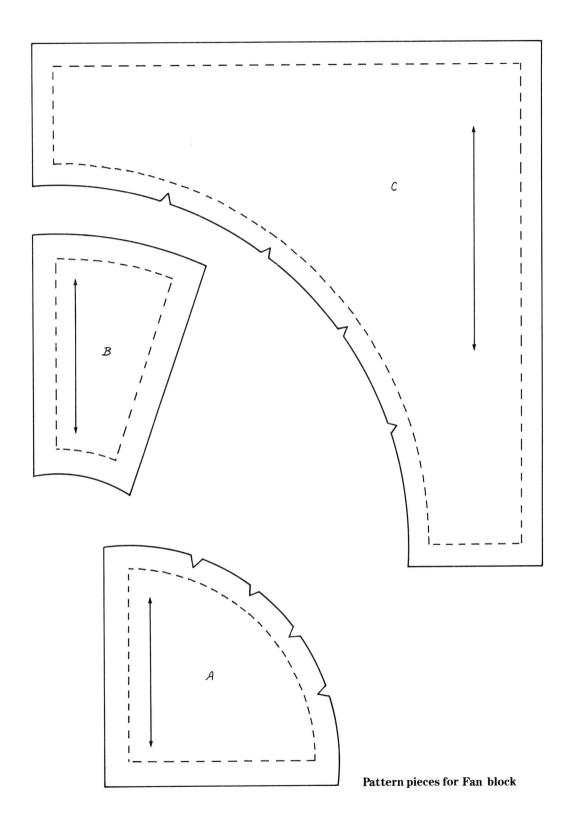

Pattern pieces for Fan block

Beautiful Borders

Expert quilters take pride in devising intricately pieced or appliquéd borders and sashing strips to set off the patchwork blocks on a prize quilt. But even a novice stitcher can create a beautiful frame from any patchwork design, using some of the gorgeously patterned stripes and border print fabrics that have become so popular in recent years.

For the Butterfly at the Crossroads quilt pictured here, we combined a narrow geometric stripe and a wider floral-patterned stripe from the same fabric to create sashing strips and a deep, richly patterned border. Appliquéd strips of the same patterned fabrics turn a miscellaneous collection of sheets, pillowcases, tablecloths, and terry towels into a deftly coordinated ensemble.

BUTTERFLY AT THE CROSSROADS WALL QUILT

The quilt consists of six 12½ × 12½-inch pattern blocks arranged in 2 rows of 3 blocks each. The blocks are separated by 1½-inch-wide sashing strips and framed by a 6-inch-wide border pieced from 3 different bands of patterned stripes. The finished size of the wall quilt is approximately 39 × 53 inches.

Materials

1⅔ yards muslin or white fabric (includes backing)
¾ yard blue or other solid-color fabric for pattern squares
2 yards (approximately) patterned stripe fabric for sashing and borders (the amount of striped fabric required depends on the pattern of the stripes; excess fabric can be used for appliqué trim on coordinated projects)
39 × 53-inch rectangle of batting
5½ yards contrasting bias binding
cardboard or plastic for templates

Directions

1. Trace patterns and make templates for each of the 3 pattern pieces on page 85 (patterns include ¼-inch seam allowances).

2. Trace and cut out the following fabric pieces:

from white fabric:
   (A) 24 squares
   (B) 48 triangles
   (C) 24 rectangles

from blue fabric:
   (A) 30 squares
   (B) 48 triangles

from striped fabric:
   approximately 13 yards (total) of 2-inch-wide patterned stripes (for 1½-inch-wide finished strips)
   approximately 5½ yards (total) of 3½-inch-wide patterned stripes (for 3-inch-wide finished strips)

3. Piece 6 pattern blocks as shown in Figure 1.

To Assemble the Quilt Top

1. Refer to assembly diagram (Figure 2). Pin and stitch two 2 × 13-inch sashing strips between 3 pattern blocks (¼-inch seams). Repeat to join a second set of 3 blocks.

2. Pin and stitch a 2 × 40½-inch sashing strip between the two 3-block strips.

3. Stitch a 2-inch-wide border strip to each short end of the quilt (sides), and then stitch a similar strip to the top and one to the bottom of the pieced design; miter corners (i.e., join border strips on the diagonal where they meet at corners).

4. Pin and stitch 3½-inch-wide border strips (3-inch-wide finished size) to the pieced center panel; miter corners. Trim this second border strip with a third and final band of narrow patterned strips (1½-inches-wide finished size) to complete the 6-inch-wide borders.

5. Back the pieced top with matching rectangles of batting and backing fabric. Baste all 3 layers together. Quilt as desired.

6. Trim raw edges even with the pieced top. Bind the edges with narrow, contrasting strips of bias binding.

7. Mount the quilt for hanging (see page 44 for tips on hanging quilts).

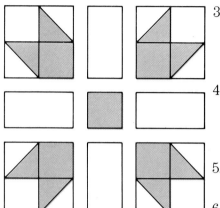

Figure 1. Assembly diagram for one Butterfly at the Crossroads block

Figure 2. Assembly diagram for Butterfly at the Crossroads wall quilt

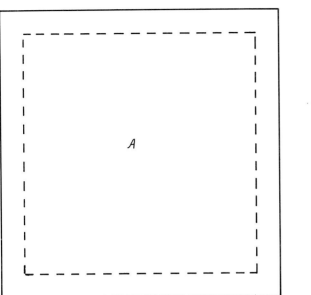

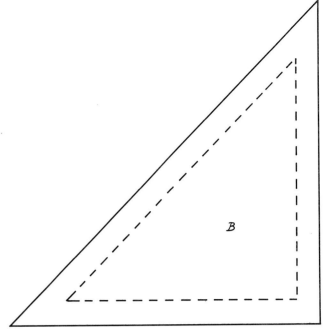

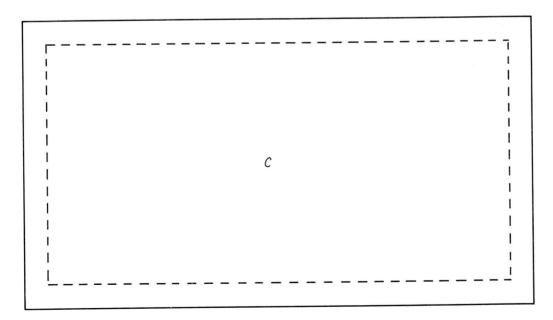

Pattern pieces for Butterfly at the Crossroads block

COORDINATED DESIGNS FOR BED AND BATH

To coordinate bed and bath linens with the patchwork wall quilt, appliqué matching strip cut from striped fabric to one or more of the following items. (Be sure to prewash all border fabrics before applying to sheets or other items that will be laundered regularly.)

Sheets and Pillowcases

Cut patterned stripes of various widths. Turn under raw edges ¼ inch on long sides of each fabric strip and press. Pin and topstitch one or more bands of patterned stripe fabric along the flat or ruffled hems of purchased sheets and pillowcases. Appliqué the stripes from edge to edge on sheets (piece strips if necessary) and from seam to seam on pillowcases.

Throw Pillows

Trim pieced or plain pillows with borders and/or ruffles made from patterned stripe fabric.

Tablecloth

Cut a 36-inch square of solid or print fabric for the basic cloth. Then cut 6 strips of patterned stripe fabric, each 1½ to 2 inches wide and 36 inches long. Press under raw edges ¼ inch on the long sides of each strip. Then arrange the strips in a lattice pattern across the top of the cloth, as shown in Figure 3. Pin and topstitch strips in place. Fold raw edges of each side of square over ¼ inch, right sides together, and press.

Cut 4 border strips of patterned stripe fabric, each 3½ × 36½ inches. Press under ¼ inch on long edges of each strip. Pin and topstitch 1 border strip to each side of the cloth; miter corners.

Embellished Towels

Bands of patterned stripe fabric combined with lace and woven ribbon trim turn inexpensive terry towels into custom bath accessories. Cut patterned stripes of various widths to required length (width of towel plus ¼ inch on each end for seam allowance). Press under raw edges and pin and topstitch stripes in place, along with bands of lace and woven ribbon, if desired. Refer to photo for suggestions.

Hint: When stitching trims to terrycloth, loosen the tension on your sewing machine slightly, and use a fairly long stitch to topstitch the trims in place. Ease the trim slightly as you stitch so that, when the towels are folded on a rack, the trim will lie flat.

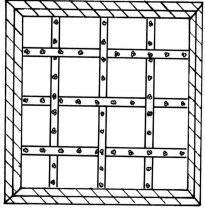

Figure 3. Assembly diagram for latticework tablecloth

REVERSE APPLIQUÉ ROSE QUILT

The pattern blocks for this handsome wall hanging came from Massachusetts textile specialist Lynne Weaver. Neither she nor I had ever come across a design quite like this block before. The pattern is cut from a single piece of folded paper, much as a child cuts out a paper snowflake. The technique is similar to that used for Hawaiian appliqué quilts, but this particular pattern was quite new to me, and I was intrigued by the way the blossom and leaves take shape from negative — or cutout — shapes in the appliqué piece, so that the appliqué actually resembles a stencil pattern.

The method of construction for each block is also a bit unusual: Each appliqué piece is stitched through 3 layers — muslin background, fleece or cotton batting, and muslin backing — so that the whipstitching that tacks the appliqué in place also creates a quilted pattern on the reverse side of the block. I'm not sure when or where these blocks were pieced, but this seems to be an early version of the now-popular "quilt-as-you-go" technique — a timesaving method in which each pattern block is appliquéd and quilted in a single step. Instructions for the quilt-as-you-go method of construction are included in the directions that follow, but you can also appliqué the designs to muslin blocks and then piece, back, and quilt the design in the traditional manner, if you prefer. The finished wall hanging measures approximately 46 inches square.

Materials

3 yards muslin for front and backing of blocks
1¼ yards yellow/gold fabric for appliqués
⅔ yard contrasting print for sashing and borders
5¼ yards contrasting bias binding (optional)
flannel-weight polyester fleece or cotton batting (about 45 × 60 inches)
16-inch square of tracing paper and plastic or cardboard for templates

Directions

1. To make a complete pattern: Fold the square of tracing paper into fourths. Trace the quarter pattern for the Reverse Appliqué Rose design (page 91) onto one quarter of the folded paper, placing dotted lines along folds in the paper, as indicated on the pattern. Cut out the traced pattern from folded paper, unfold the completed pattern, and press gently with a warm iron. Transfer the paper design to plastic or cardboard and cut out a template. *Note:* Template does *not* include seam allowances.

2. Cut nine 13 × 13-inch squares of yellow/gold fabric. Center and trace one rose design on the *right* side of each square.

3. Cut out the appliqué shapes, leaving just about ⅛-inch seam allowance beyond the traced lines (omit seam allowances for machine appliqué). Clip all seams at regular intervals up to the traced stitching line.

4. Cut eighteen 15 × 15-inch squares of muslin and 9 matching squares of fleece or cotton batting. Sandwich 1 square of fleece between 2 muslin squares and baste around all 4 edges. Repeat to make 9 quilt squares.

5. Locate and mark the center of each muslin square (see pages 23–24). Center and baste 1 appliqué cutout on each muslin block. Baste all around the appliqué shape about ¼ inch inside the traced stitching lines.

6. Appliqué 1 rose shape to each block, taking tiny, even whipstitches through all 4 layers of fabric (folded edge of the appliqué, muslin background, batting, and muslin backing). Use your fingers and the tip of your needle to coax the seam allowance under as you stitch (see pages 23–27 for appliqué details). Appliqué all 9 blocks.

To Join the Blocks:

1. Lift and peel back the front and back muslin squares and trim the batting ¼ inch around the edges on each block. Turn under the raw edges of the top and bottom layers of muslin ¼ inch and press. Repeat for each block.

2. Lay 2 blocks edge to edge and whipstitch together along the front and back seams (see Figure 1). Continue stitching blocks together to form 3 rows of 3 blocks each. Then use the same technique to join the 3 rows together to complete the quilt top.

For Sashing and Borders:

1. Cut four 2 × 45-inch strips of sashing fabric. Press long edges under ¼ inch on each strip.

2. Pin and stitch 1 sashing strip over each of the 2 vertical seams in the quilt (trim the length if necessary). Next, pin and stitch 1 strip over each of the 2 horizontal seams in the quilt (see Figure 2).

3. For borders, cut 4 strips of sashing and border fabric, each 3½ × 47 inches (piece if necessary). Also cut 4 matching strips of flannel-weight batting. Center, pin, and baste a strip of batting to the *wrong* side of each border strip.

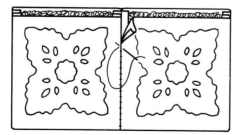

Figure 1. Whipstitch quilted blocks together

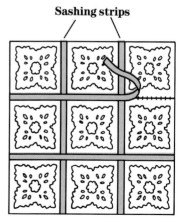

Sashing strips

Figure 2. Assembly diagram for Reverse Appliqué Rose quilt

4. With right sides facing, position and pin the edge of 1 border strip about ¾ inch in from the edge of 1 side of the quilt . Machine stitch the border strip to the quilt (¼ inch seams). Fold the border to the back of the quilt, turn under the raw edge ¼ inch, and slip-stitch the border to the backing. Press. Repeat for the border on the opposite side of the quilt. Trim the ends of each side border strip even with the top and bottom edges of the quilt.

5. For the top and bottom borders, position and pin the 2 remaining border strips to the remaining sides of the quilt top, as described in step 4, above. Stitch the borders in place, fold to the back, turn under raw edges, and stitch to the backing along seam lines. Turn in the raw edges at the ends of the top and bottom border strips and slip-stitch the seams closed.

6. If you like, outline the edges of the border with narrow strips of bias binding in a contrasting color picked up from the print used for the sashing and border strips.

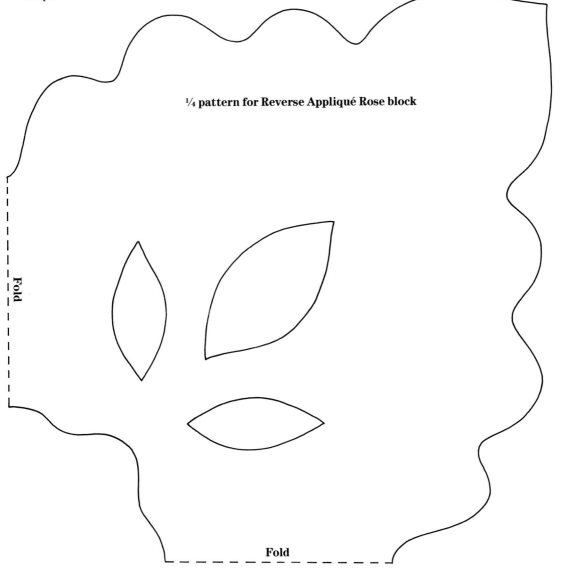

¼ pattern for Reverse Appliqué Rose block

Fold

Fold

Christmas Delights

The holidays, it seems, are always just around the corner. Here's a dazzling array of patchwork ornaments and Christmas accessories in honor of the season.

Galaxy of Star Trims

Here's a shower of patchwork star ornaments to trim your tree or stitch as gifts.

MEMORY STAR ORNAMENTS

The stars on the preceding pages are stitched from a variety of festive fabrics. However, one family I know creates a new batch of ornaments each Christmas from the most unlikely materials. Some are made for their own tree and others are created as personalized ornament gifts for special friends, but each star is designed to commemorate a significant event of the year just past. For these one-of-a-kind stars, the family selects fabrics reminiscent of a special event or an individual. Last year their tree featured stars made of every kind of fabric from wedding lace to baby bunting, including samples stitched from grey flannel, denim, and prom-night taffeta. Often it turns out that the humbler or more unexpected the fabric, the more treasured the ornament.

Backing each star with muslin or a solid-color cotton provides space for writing or embroidering good wishes or relevant information on the back of each ornament — a date or name or occasion — so that you can recall each happy event and special friend when the stars are brought out to trim the tree every year. Embellish each star with bits of trim, beading, lace or buttons as fancy dictates (refer to the color photo on pages 92–93 for ideas).

On page 97 are full-size patterns for 5-point (*A*) and 6-point (*B*) stars. The smaller diamond in each case is used for cutting and piecing star ornaments, while the larger pattern is used for cutting and piecing a larger treetop ornament.

Materials

scraps of festive fabrics in your choice of colors, including some light and some dark
fiber fill for stuffing
muslin or solid-color cotton fabric for backing (optional)
ribbons, lace, buttons, and decorative cording for trim (optional)
gold thread for hanging
cardboard or plastic for templates
fine-point permanent fabric-marking pen
narrow grosgrain ribbon (for treetop ornaments)

Directions

Note: Patterns do *not* include seam allowances.

Five-point Star

Note: The finished ornament measures approximately 5 inches, point to point.

1. Trace the small diamond pattern piece (*A*), add ¼-inch seam allowances to the piece and cut a template from cardboard or plastic.
2. For each star, trace and cut 5 of piece (*A*) from mixed or matching fabrics.

3. With right sides facing, pin and stitch 2 diamonds together along 1 short side, stitching only from seam line to seam line, as shown in Figure 1. Do not stitch into the seam allowance or you will have difficulty pressing the seam allowances flat when the star is completed. One by one, pin and stitch the 3 remaining diamonds to the first pair to complete one 5-point star. Press the seams in one direction all the way around the star on the *wrong* side. The points meeting in the center should lie flat.

4. With right sides facing, lay the pieced star on a scrap of muslin or other backing fabric and trace around the star onto the fabric. Cut out the backing shape.

5. With right sides still facing, stitch the pieced star to the backing around 5 points, leaving an opening between 2 points for turning and stuffing. Trim the points, clip the corners and angles, turn the star right side out, and press.

6. Stuff the star ornament firmly with fiber fill. A blunt knitting needle or similar implement is useful for pushing stuffing into each point of the star. Slip-stitch the opening closed.

7. Embellish the star with buttons, lace appliqués, or other trim, if desired (refer to the color photo for ideas). Write a message and date on the back of each star with indelible fabric marker, or embroider the information with a simple outline stitch, if you prefer. (See page 36 for stitch diagram.) Add a loop of gold thread to the tip of 1 point of the star for hanging.

Six-point Star

Note: The finished ornament measures approximately 4½ inches, point to point.

1. Trace and cut out a template for small diamond shape (*B*). Add ¼-inch seam allowances to the template.

2. For each ornament, trace and cut 6 of piece (B), cutting 3 pieces from each of 2 different fabrics (one light and one dark).

3. To construct a 6-point star, pin 1 light and 1 dark diamond together with right sides facing. Stitch the 2 diamonds together along the seam line on 1 side, stitching from seam line to seam line only (do not stitch into the seam allowance). Make 3 identical pairs of diamonds, then pin and stitch the 3 pairs together to complete the star, as shown in Figure 2. Press seams in one direction.

4. As described in step 4 above, trace and back the star with muslin or other fabric. Turn, press, stuff, and trim the ornament as described for the 5-point star.

Treetop Stars

Note: The 5-point treetop star measures approximately 9 inches, point to point; the 6-point treetop star measures 8 inches, point to point.

1. Trace and cut a template for the larger diamond shape: (*A*) for a 5-point star or (*B*) for a 6-point star. Add ¼-inch seam allowances to each template.

2. Cut and piece the star as described for the ornaments. Striped fabrics were used to create the 5-point treetop star pictured here.

3. Trim the star with decorative cording, if desired, and stitch a circle of lace and a fancy button to the center of the star, drawing thread from front to back and securing it so that the button makes a gentle indentation in the stuffed star.

4. Fold a 10-inch strip of narrow grosgrain ribbon in half and tack the center of the ribbon to the center back of the pieced star. Use the ribbon to tie the star to the top of the Christmas tree (see Figure 3).

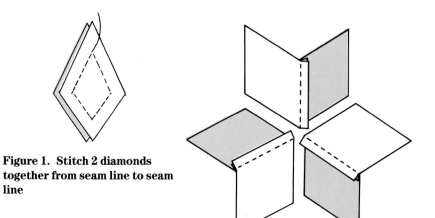

Figure 1. Stitch 2 diamonds together from seam line to seam line

Figure 2. Assembling a 6-point star

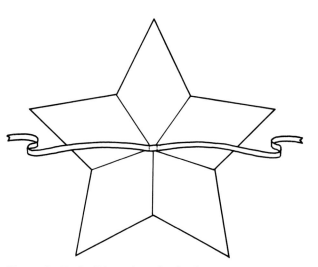

Figure 3. Tack ribbon tie to back of treetop ornament

Pattern pieces for 5-point star

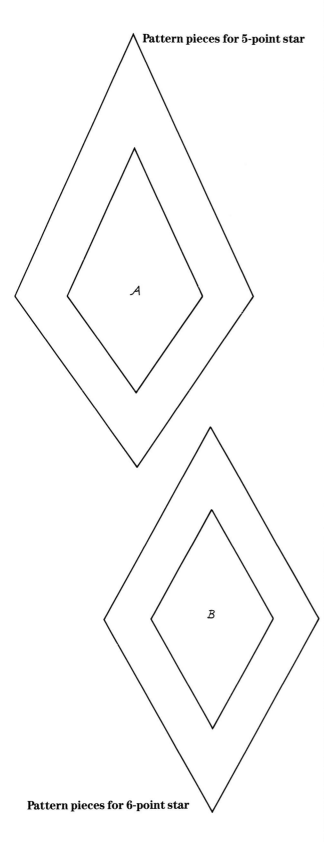

A

B

Pattern pieces for 6-point star

Holiday Table Setting

Pieced 8-point stars, appliquéd to background squares and framed with bands of contrasting fabric, make perfect dessert place mats for a holiday party. With timesaving strip-piecing methods and speedy machine appliqué, you can stitch a set of 8 mats in a weekend and still have time to piece a large star-shaped doily for the center of your table.

Note: For quick piecing, these mats are neither lined nor quilted, but feel free to add a layer of batting and backing to each mat if you have the time and inclination.

STAR PLACE MATS

Materials and directions are for a set of eight 13 × 13-inch mats.

Materials

½ yard *each* of a light and a dark fabric (solids or prints) for star appliqués
1¼ yards contrasting background fabric
1¼ yards striped border fabric
cardboard or plastic for template

Directions

1. Trace and cut a template for the full-size diamond pattern piece on page 100 (pattern is shown actual size for place mat stars and half the actual size for centerpiece star). Add ¼-inch seam allowances to the diamond template.

2. For each star mat, cut 1 strip of light fabric and 1 of dark, each 2¾ × 18 inches. With right sides facing, place the light strip on top of the dark strip and stitch the 2 strips together along the right-hand side (¼-inch seams). Press the strip, but do not open the seam.

3. Lay the template on the light side of the strip, matching the edges of template with the raw edges of fabric as shown in Figure 1. Mark the top and bottom cutting lines diagonally across the strip. Reposition the template and mark again, moving the template down the strip until you have marked off 4 diamond shapes.

4. Cut diamond shapes from the strip. Open each pair of diamonds and press the seam to one side, toward the darker fabric. Pin and stitch the 4 diamond pairs together to form one 8-point star (see Figure 2). Press.

5. Press under ¼-inch seam allowances along each star point. Position 1 pieced star on the center of a 13-inch square of contrasting background fabric. Pin star to backing and topstitch ⅛ inch in from the folded edges of the points.

6. Cut 2½-inch-wide strips of striped fabric for the borders. With the right sides facing, pin and stitch border strips 1½ inches in from the raw edges on either side of the mat, just touching the points of the star appliqué. Fold the excess border fabric to the back of the mat and slip-stitch in place on the backing. Repeat for the top and bottom edges of the mat; miter corners neatly.

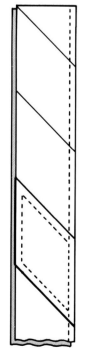

Figure 1. Mark and cut diamonds from pieced strips

STAR CENTERPIECE

The finished doily measures approximately 20 inches in diameter, and works particularly well for the center of a round or oval table.

Materials

¼ yard *each* of a light and a dark fabric
⅔ yard backing fabric
lace or cording trim (optional)
cardboard or plastic for template

Directions

1. Enlarge the diamond pattern piece on this page to desired size. Trace the shape and cut a template, adding ¼-inch seam allowances.

2. Trace and cut 4 light and 4 dark diamonds. Pin and stitch the diamonds into 4 identical pairs of 1 light and 1 dark shape each. Always stitch pairs with the light diamond on top.

3. Stitch the 4 pairs of diamonds together to complete the 8-point star (do *not* stitch into the seam allowance; stitch from seam to seam only). See Figure 2. Press seams to one side and press the center of the star flat.

4. Trace and cut out a matching, star-shaped piece of backing fabric. With right sides facing, pin the back and front of the star together. Stitch around all 8 points, leaving an opening between 2 points for turning. Clip seams, trim points, turn star right side out, and press. Slip-stitch the opening closed.

5. Machine stitch ¼ inch in from seam lines on each star point to tack the backing and pieced front together. Hand or machine appliqué a narrow edging of lace or decorative cording around the edges of the star, if desired.

Each square equals 2 inches

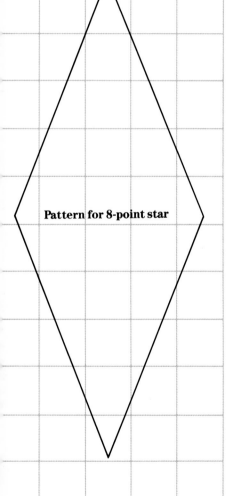

Pattern for 8-point star

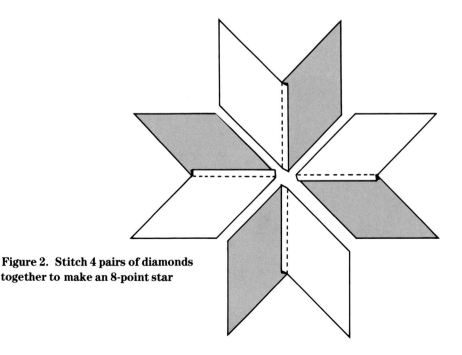

Figure 2. Stitch 4 pairs of diamonds together to make an 8-point star

100

String-Pieced Designs

The easy-to-make stocking and heart-shaped ornaments shown on the next page have the look of old-fashioned crazy quilt pieces, but they're actually cut and stitched from string patchwork fabric — narrow strips of fabric that have been randomly pieced together on the sewing machine to create a new patchwork fabric. The hearts are cut from string-pieced fabric and the stocking is made by machine stitching strings of fabric directly onto a stocking-shaped muslin base. String patchwork can be pieced from any kind of fabric, but for best results keep fabrics of similar weight and fiber content together (piece cottons with cottons, silks with silks, and wools with wools, for example).

PATCHWORK HEART ORNAMENTS

Materials

narrow fabric strips in various widths, from ½ to 1½ inches wide, and about 18
 inches long (piece strips if necessary)
fiber fill
cardboard or plastic for templates
decorative cording (optional)
gold thread or narrow ribbon

Directions

1. Sort the fabric into piles by color and then divide the color piles into prints and solids, with separate piles for miscellaneous, plaids, and multiple-color prints. This will enable you to see at a glance the materials you have to choose from as you sew.

2. Cut and piece fabric into strips of a similar length (about 18 inches each). With right sides facing, machine stitch the strips together, one after another, as shown in Figure 1, angling some strips as you piece to create a more dynamic surface pattern. Continue adding strips until you have a strip-pieced square of fabric about 18 × 18 inches.

3. Press the completed patchwork fabric carefully (to avoid stretching it); press all seams in the same direction.

4. Trace and cut a template for the heart pattern on page 103 (pattern includes ¼-inch seam allowances).

5. Trace and cut out 2 heart shapes from the string-pieced fabric (as shown in Figure 2) for each ornament. With right sides facing, stitch the hearts together, leaving an opening along 1 side for turning. Trim seams, clip curves, turn the heart right side out, and press.

6. Stuff the heart lightly with fiber fill and slip-stitch the opening closed. Trim the edges of each ornament with purchased cording and add a loop of gold thread or narrow ribbon for hanging.

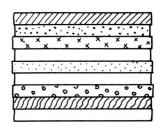

Figure 1. Stitch strips together to create new fabric yardage

Figure 2. Trace and cut heart shapes from string-pieced fabric

101

Pattern for heart-shaped string patchwork ornaments

HEIRLOOM STOCKING

The stocking may be cut from string-pieced fabric, as previously described for the heart ornaments, but the pressed piecing method of construction described below actually creates a more interesting design for larger projects like the stocking or a pillow top.

Materials

narrow fabric strips in assorted widths
½ yard muslin for backing
½ yard contrasting fabric for lining
⅓ yard plain fabric for stocking back (optional)
½ yard ruffled fabric or lace for cuff *or* decorative cording or ribbon (optional)

Directions

1. Enlarge the stocking pattern to desired size and cut 2 shapes from muslin or other backing fabric (add ¼-inch seam allowances to each piece). Also, cut matching shapes from lining fabric.

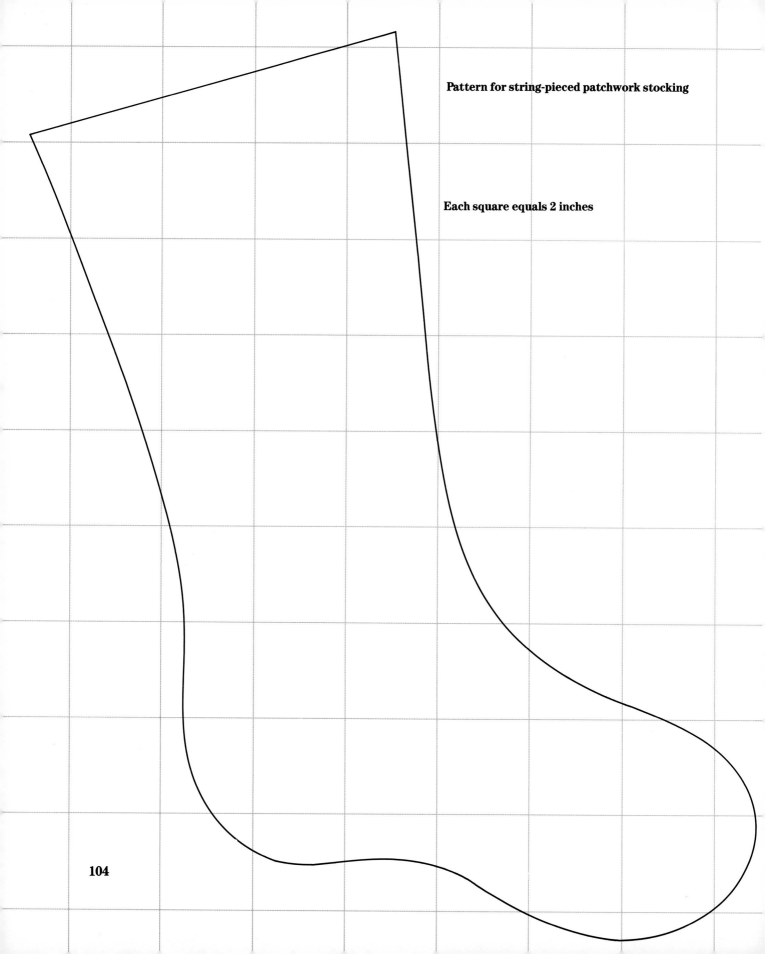

Pattern for string-pieced patchwork stocking

Each square equals 2 inches

104

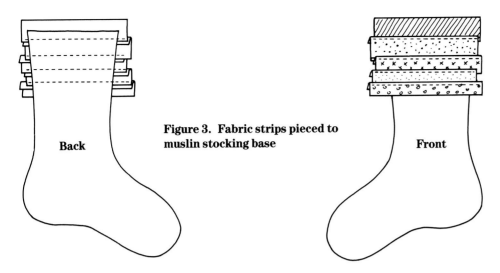

Figure 3. Fabric strips pieced to muslin stocking base

Back

Front

2. Beginning at the top of the muslin shape, stitch a fabric strip across the top of the stocking. As with crazy quilt patching (see pages 32–34), the edges of the string patches should extend slightly beyond the edges of the muslin base; the excess fabric will be trimmed away later.

3. With right sides facing, position and stitch a second strip over the first, as shown in Figure 3. Smooth this second strip down and press. Continue to add fabric strips, angling the strips up or down from time to time as you move down the stocking and around the heel toward the toe. Finger-press after each strip is added so that the strings will lie flat against the backing fabric.

4. When the surface of the stocking shape is completely covered with string patchwork, trim the edges even with the muslin backing and baste around the edges of the stocking to secure the strips.

5. Make a matching string-pieced shape for the back of the stocking, or cut the back from contrasting fabric. With right sides facing, pin the back and front of the stocking together and stitch around the sides, leaving the top open for turning. Trim seams, clip curves, turn the stocking right side out, and press.

6. To finish the stocking: Pin and stitch a ruffle of lace or fabric or a row of decorative cording along the top of the stocking. Press the seam toward the inside of the stocking. With right sides together, pin and stitch the back and front lining together. Trim the seam and slip the lining inside the completed patchwork stocking, turn under raw edges along top and slip-stitch in place. Add a loop of ribbon or cording so the stocking can be hung.

Cut-And-Paste Christmas Cards

Patchwork cards like those on the next page require no stitching, but they're a wonderful way to use up fabric scraps and create any-occasion greeting cards that can also be framed as mini-gifts.

Materials

scraps of lightweight cotton or satiny fabrics
lightweight iron-on interfacing
fabric glue or rubber cement or white glue
plain purchased cards and matching envelopes (available in stationery stores)
gold and silver or other colorful markers (available in art supply shops)
scraps of narrow ribbon for trim (optional)
cardboard or plastic for templates

Directions

1. Trace patterns for 5- and 6-point stars (page 97), omitting seam allowances. Or trace the pattern pieces for patchwork motifs of your choice from among those shown here or from other sources. Cut out templates for each pattern piece. Do *not* add seam allowances.

2. Fuse a piece of lightweight iron-on interfacing to the backs of the assorted fabric scraps to stabilize the fabric and prevent ravelling.

3. Trace and cut out pattern pieces for each patchwork design from the fabrics of your choice. Arrange the pattern pieces for each design on the front of a plain, purchased card; glue the pieces in place with fabric glue or rubber cement.

4. Embellish with colored or metallic markers and bits of ribbon or trim, as desired. Write a message inside and send the card to a friend.

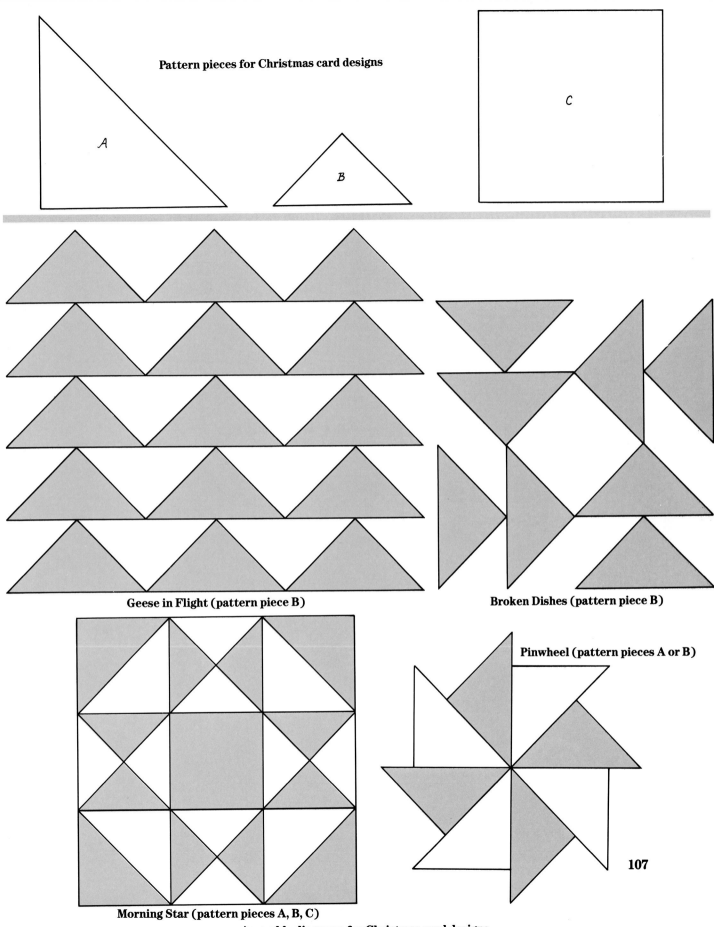

Pattern pieces for Christmas card designs

A

B

C

Geese in Flight (pattern piece B)

Broken Dishes (pattern piece B)

Pinwheel (pattern pieces A or B)

Morning Star (pattern pieces A, B, C)

Assembly diagrams for Christmas card designs

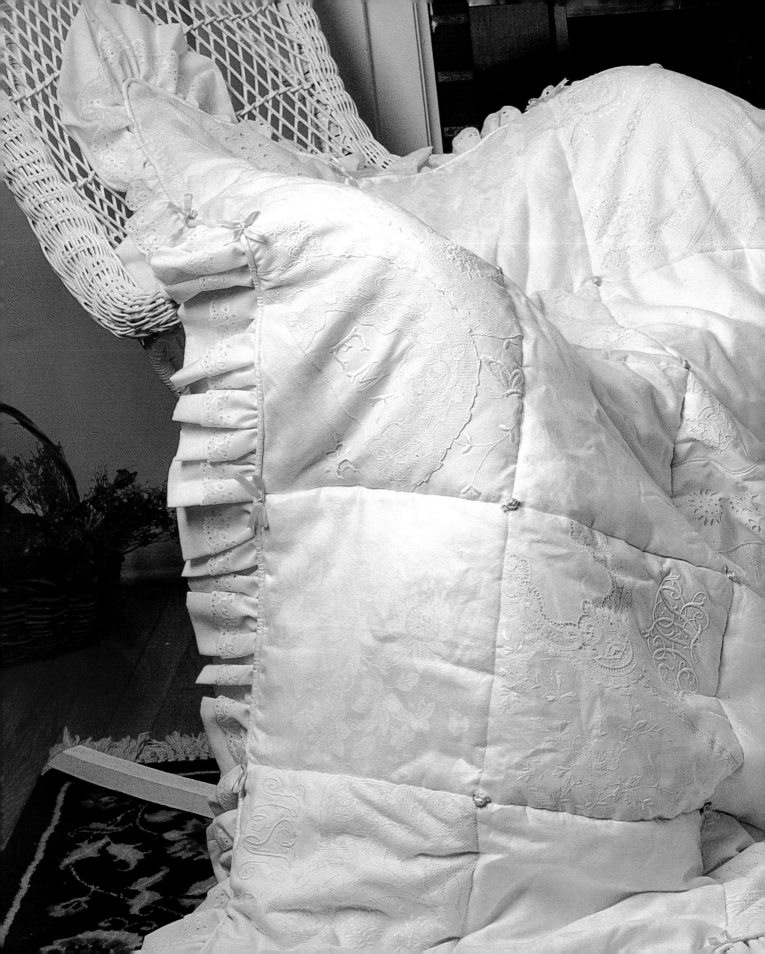

Quilts to Cherish

On the following pages you'll find a selection of very special quilts to make. Some are traditional patterns, others are the creations of contemporary quilters. Each design awaits your personal interpretation.

LACE COLLAGE COVERLET

With clever cutting and expert piecing in the crazy quilt tradition, designer Carol Franklin of Peterborough, New Hampshire, creates wonderfully romantic, one-of-a-kind quilts and pillows from scraps of lace and damask linen. For a magazine story on patchwork with a "Victorian" flavor, I adapted the luxurious lace coverlet and pillow pictured on the preceding pages from one of Carol's original designs.

Most of the embroidered and monogrammed materials for the collage squares were contributed by our mutual friend, lace expert Sallie McIntosh, who had lovingly salvaged and stashed such beautiful oddments for years with just such a project in mind. I hope both Carol and Sally are as pleased with the results of this collaborative effort as I am.

The 60 × 60-inch coverlet consists of alternating blocks of patchwork lace and plain damask linen arranged in 5 rows of five 12-inch squares each. The quilt is finished with a flirty double ruffle of linen and lace.

I hasten to point out that Carol uses only scraps from damaged pieces to create her elegant lace squares. After all, rescuing what might have been discarded, and stitching it into something unique and new and beautiful, is half the pleasure and much of the artistry in a patchwork project like this one.

Materials

1¾ yards lightweight white fabric for lining lace squares
2 to 3 yards (total) assorted lace scraps (monograms and embroidered linens contribute to the rich texture of the finished collage squares)
1¾ yards damask linen or other white-on-white fabric
3½ yards white fabric for quilt backing
3 yards lightweight white linen or cotton fabric for ruffle
17 yards 2½ to 3-inch-wide lace for inner ruffle
7½ yards white fabric-covered cording (optional)
16 small satin bows and/or 16 small purchased rosettes (optional)
60-inch square of batting

Directions

Note: All measurements include ¼-inch seam allowances.

1. To prepare lace for appliqué, wash all pieces by hand in a mild detergent. Rinse the lace thoroughly, dry, and press each piece with a warm iron. (*Note:* A light coating of starch will make the lace easier to appliqué.) Discard pieces that are badly stained or otherwise unusable. Mend small tears and ravels in other sections to increase usable surface. Fine lace is precious, so be thrifty — *and* creative!

2. Cut thirteen 12½-inch squares of lightweight white fabric as a lining for the lace collage blocks. Cut and position pieces of lace on each square, working from one corner toward the opposite corner, or from the center of the square out toward the edges. Mix scale and types of lace on each square to add visual

and textural interest. Study closely the collage blocks on the pillow top (pictured on pages 108–109) for ideas.

To Appliqué the Squares:

1. Pin and baste all pieces in place. Whenever possible, position finished edges of lace pieces to overlap cut edges. Overlap edges no more than ¼ inch from piece to piece, and make sure that raw or uneven edges are neatly trimmed where they are visible beneath overlapping pieces.

2. Wherever the raw edges of 1 piece of lace or fabric overlaps another piece, fold under the raw edge of the top piece slightly and appliqué, stitching through all layers of the fabric, including the lining fabric.

3. Appliqué pieces by machine or by hand, using tiny overcast stitches taken very close together, to reinforce fragile lace edges. (For more on lace appliqué, see pages 34–36.)

4. Piece a total of thirteen lace collage squares. Trim the edges of the lace appliqués to match the edges of the lining squares.

To Assemble the Quilt Top:

1. Cut twelve 12½-inch squares of damask linen. Arrange the 12 linen and 13 lace squares in 5 rows of 5 squares each, alternating linen and lace blocks. Stitch the blocks into rows, then stitch the rows together to make the quilt top. Use ¼-inch seams throughout; press seams toward the lace blocks.

2. If desired, pin and stitch a length of fabric-covered cording ⅜ inch in from the raw edges of the quilt top.

3. Cut and piece an 8 × 580-inch strip of lightweight linen or cotton fabric for the ruffle. Sew the short ends together, fold the strip in half lengthwise (wrong sides together), and press. Pin and baste a matching length of lace along the raw edges of the ruffle strip. Gather this double ruffle to fit the quilt top. Pin and stitch in place, using the zipper foot on your sewing machine. (See pages 41–42 for details on cording and ruffles.)

4. Cut and piece the backing to size. Trim batting to ½ inch smaller than the quilt top on all sides. Center and baste the backing, batting, and pieced top together.

5. Turn under the raw edges of the backing and slip-stitch to the back of the ruffle, along the seam line.

6. Quilt along seam lines between blocks by hand or machine. Pin or stitch small satin bows and/or purchased rosettes at the intersection of each corner, if desired.

LACE COLLAGE PILLOW

1. Cut and piece four 12½-inch lace collage squares, as described for the coverlet. Stitch the squares together to form a larger square, using ¼-inch seams.

2. Back the pieced top with a layer of batting and a square of lining fabric; quilt along the seams between the blocks, stitching through all 3 layers.

3. Finish the edges of the pillow top with cording and a double ruffle of fabric and lace, as described for the coverlet.

4. Back the pillow with white damask fabric, trim the corners and seams, turn, and press. Stuff the pillow with fiber fill or a 24-inch purchased pillow form; slip-stitch the bottom closed.

5. Sew a lace-covered button to the center of the pillow if desired.

IRISH CHAIN WEEKEND QUILT

Happily, it isn't always necessary to spend long hours of cutting and piecing to make a beautiful quilt. Using speedy strip-piecing techniques, you can stitch and piece the traditional Irish Chain pattern, right, over a weekend.

Much of the charm of this quilt lies in the subtle mix of fabrics — large- and small-scale prints in the same soft shades of blue and cream. For a bolder look, choose one dark and one light solid-color fabric, or a solid and a print in colors of your choice.

The Irish Chain quilt is composed of 10½-inch squares. Strip-pieced, 9-patch pattern blocks alternate with plain squares to form 9 horizontal rows of 7 squares each. The finished quilt is bound with bias strips and measures approximately 73½ × 94½ inches — suitable for a single or double-size bed.

Materials

Note: Yardages are based on 45-inch fabrics.

(A) — 1⅔ yards large-scale floral print (dark fabric)
(B) — 2⅔ yards small-scale floral print (light fabric)
5 yards matching or contrasting fabric for backing
9 yards bias binding in matching or contrasting color
    medium-weight batting

Directions

Note: All measurements include ¼-inch seam allowances.

1. Cut the following:
from (A):
    15 strips, each 4 × 45 inches (cut across width of fabric)
from (B):
    12 strips, each 4 × 45 inches (cut across width of fabric)
    31 squares, each 11 × 11 inches

2. Pin and stitch 1 strip of fabric (B) between 2 strips of fabric (A) — see Figure 1(a). Piece a total of 6 of these strips. Press the seams open.

3. Now piece and stitch 1 strip of fabric (A) between 2 strips of fabric (B) — see Figure 1(b). Stitch a total of 3 of these strips. Press the seams open.

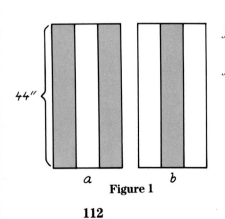

44″ {

a   b
Figure 1

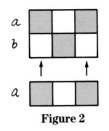

Figure 2

4. Lay the pieced strips out wrong side up on a flat surface. Mark off and cut each pieced strip into eleven 4-inch-wide slices (see pages 19–21 for details on marking and cutting units for strip-pieced projects). Discard 1-inch scraps on the end of each strip.

5. Refer to Figure 2. Pin and stitch 1 slice of unit (b) between 2 slices of unit (a), to form a 9-patch pattern block. Make sure that corners and seam lines match perfectly, and that there is a dark (or large-scale) print square in each corner of the block. Stitch the 3 strips together to form a square. Press the seams open. Make a total of 32 such pattern blocks. (You will have pieces for 1 extra block left over — enough to make a small pillow.)

6. Arrange the 32 pieced blocks and 31 plain blocks in 9 rows of 7 blocks each, as shown in the assembly diagram, Figure 3. Stitch the blocks in each row together and press the seams open.

7. Now pin and stitch the 9 pieced rows together to form the quilt top.

To Complete the Quilt:

1. Piece the backing to size (see page 7).

2. Layer the backing, batting, and pieced top together and baste (see page 38).

3. Quilt by machine (or by hand, if you prefer) along all seam lines between blocks.

4. Trim the backing and batting to match the quilt top. Pin and stitch matching or contrasting strips of bias binding around the quilt edges (see page 43 for details on cutting and stitching bias strips).

Figure 3. Assembly diagram for Irish Chain weekend quilt

ROSE OF SHARON WEDDING QUILT

In days gone by, a finely wrought rose-pattern quilt was considered the *pièce de résistance* of a young girl's trousseau. In that charming tradition, the beautiful Rose of Sharon quilt shown on the next page is but one of four identical coverlets pieced in the early years of this century by Rosa Walton Bennison and her sister, Dee, as wedding gifts for Rosa's 4 beloved daughters: Mary Jane, Lucille, Gwendolyn, and Anne. All 4 quilts have remained in the family, and will continue to be cherished by succeeding generations of daughters, nieces, and daughters-in-law for years to come.

The bold Rose of Sharon motif is relatively simple to appliqué and makes a handsome design block without additional embellishment. However, the exceptionally fine quilting lavished on the Bennison bridal quilts adds immeasurably to their beauty.

The coverlet is composed of 9 appliquéd blocks, set with pink sashing strips and framed with borders of white. The finished quilt measures 79 × 79 inches.

Materials

Note: Yardages are based on 45-inch-wide fabrics.

9½ yards white or off-white polished cotton for blocks, borders, and backing
⅝ yard green cotton
½ yard medium-pink cotton
1¾ yards light-pink cotton
lightweight batting
cardboard or plastic for templates

Note: Templates do *not* include ¼-inch seam allowances. Measurements for sashing and borders *do* include ¼-inch allowances.

Directions

1. Cut the following and set aside:

from white fabric (for borders):
    2 strips, each 9½ × 64 inches
    2 strips, each 9½ × 82 inches

from light-pink fabric (for sashing):
    6 strips, each 3½ × 17 inches
    4 strips, each 3½ × 58 inches
    2 strips, each 3½ × 63 inches

2. Trace full-size pattern pieces on page 118 and cut cardboard or plastic templates for each shape.

3. On *right* side of fabrics, trace around templates to mark seam lines, and then cut out the following shapes, adding ¼-inch seam allowances to each piece:

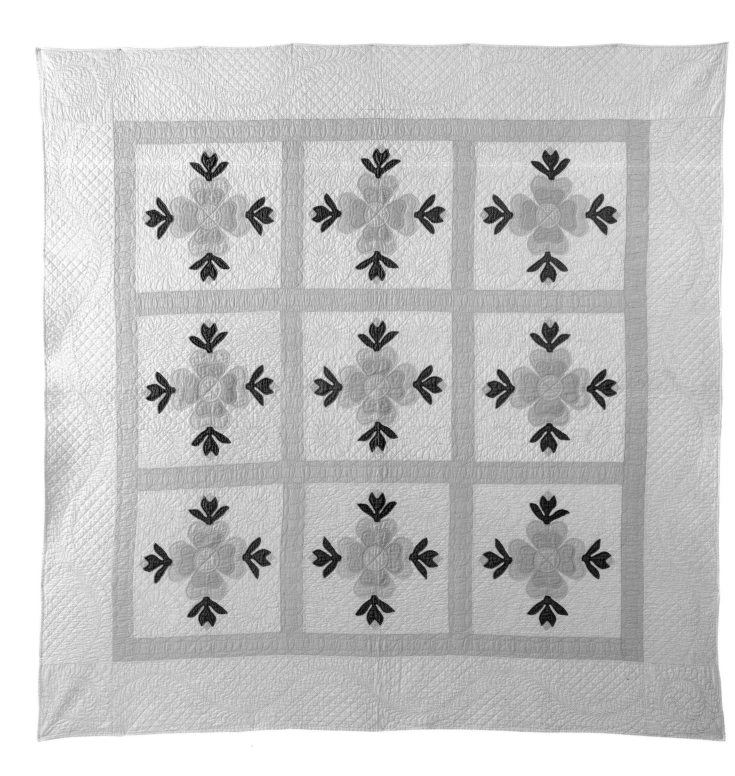

from light-pink fabric:
- (*A*) 9 pieces
- (*C*) 36 pieces
- (*E*) 36 pieces

from medium-pink fabric:
- (*B*) 36 pieces

from green fabric:
- (*D*) 36 pieces

4. Clip curves and corners and baste under the seam allowance on each appliqué piece. (Refer to pages 23–27 for appliqué details to help with steps 4–6.)

5. From white fabric, cut nine 17×17-inch blocks. Mark the horizontal and vertical center lies of each block to aid in placement of appliqués.

6. On each block, arrange 1 set of appliqué shapes as shown in the assembly diagram, Figure 1. Pin, baste, and appliqué the shapes in place. Complete a total of 9 blocks.

Each square equals 1 inch

Figure 1. Assembly diagram for Rose of Sharon quilt

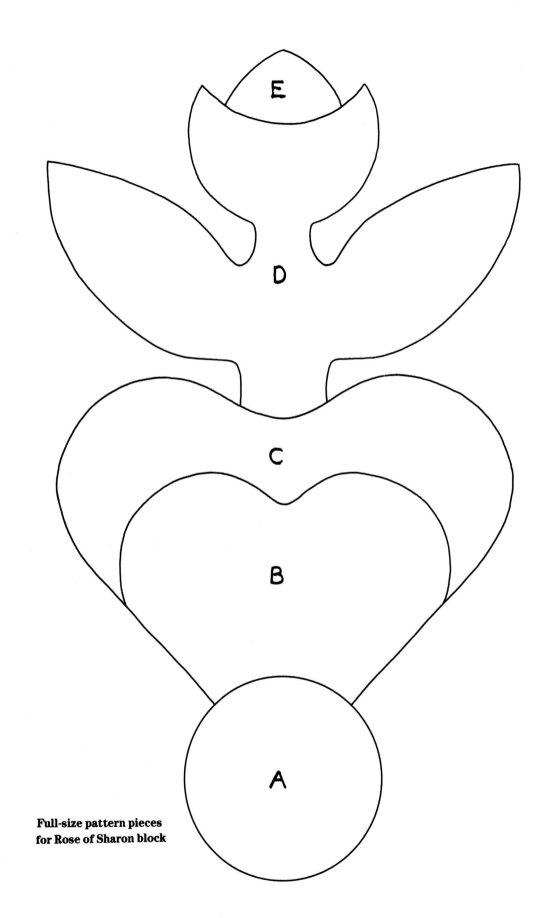

**Full-size pattern pieces
for Rose of Sharon block**

To Assemble the Quilt

1. Arrange the completed blocks in 3 rows of 3 blocks each. Pin and stitch one 3½ × 17-inch pink sashing strip between the blocks in each horizontal row (3 blocks, 2 strips per row).

2. Pin and stitch one 3½ × 58-inch pink sashing strip between each of the 3 rows, trimming the length of the strips to size as necessary. Add the 2 remaining 3½ × 58-inch pink strips to the top and bottom of the pieced rows (3 rows of blocks, 4 sashing strips). Press all seams toward the sashing strips.

3. Pin and stitch the last 2 pink sashing strips (3½ × 63 inches) to either side of the pieced top; trim length. Press all seams toward strips.

4. Pin and stitch two 9½ × 64-inch white border strips to the top and bottom of the quilt. Pin and stitch the 9½ × 82-inch white border strips to the sides of quilt (trim length as necessary). Press seams toward pink sashing.

To Finish the Quilt:

1. Cut and piece the backing to size from white fabric. Layer, pin, and baste the backing, batting, and appliquéd top together (see page 38 for details).

2. Quilt the appliquéd design in patterns of your choice, or refer to Figures 2–4 on page 120 and follow these suggestions: Outline-quilt each Rose of Sharon motif (stitch ¼ inch from seam lines). Quilt a 5-inch-diameter feathered wreath in each corner of each appliquéd block (see Figure 2) and fill the remaining space on each block with a 1-inch diamond pattern. Pink sashing strips are quilted with a design of interlocking circles (see Figure 3), and the wide white borders are embellished with a serpentine feather pattern (see Figure 4) and 1-inch channel quilting. (See pages 37–40 for more information on quilting and quilting patterns.)

3. Bind the quilt edges with 1½-inch-wide bias strips cut and pieced from the remaining white fabric.

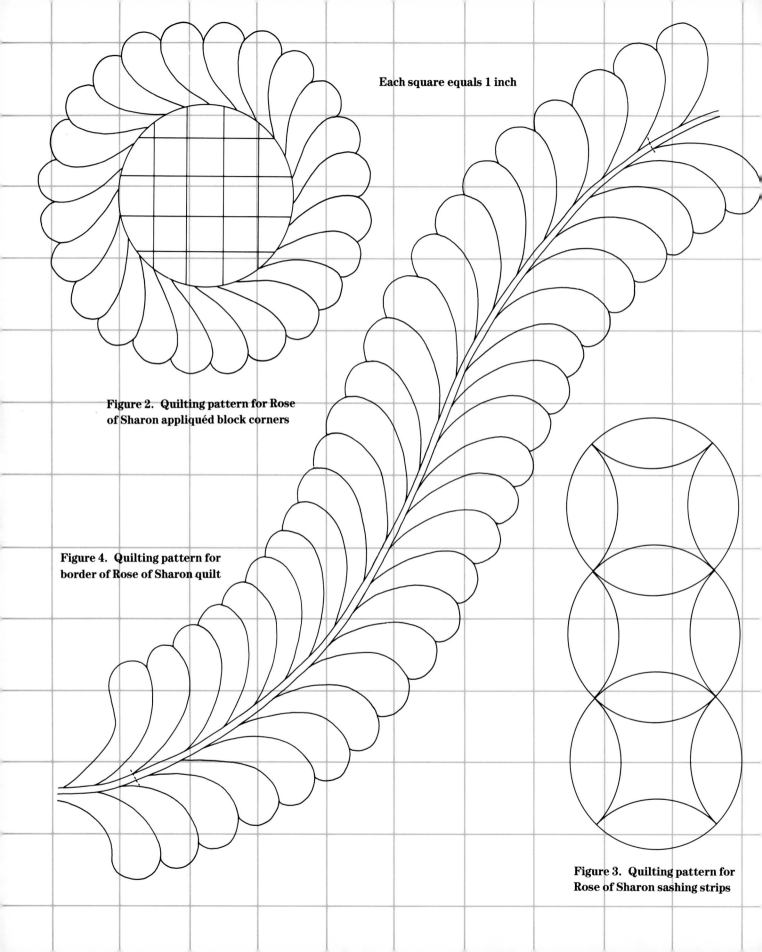

Each square equals 1 inch

Figure 2. Quilting pattern for Rose of Sharon appliquéd block corners

Figure 4. Quilting pattern for border of Rose of Sharon quilt

Figure 3. Quilting pattern for Rose of Sharon sashing strips

HEARTS AND FLOWERS CRIB QUILT

The easy-to-piece crib quilt on page 122 was inspired by the chintz print from which the patterned squares are cut—an American copy of a fabric in the textile collection of London's famed Victoria and Albert Museum. I love these delicate flower motifs, but any fabric with well-spaced, clearly defined motifs that fit comfortably within a 4½-inch square would work equally well. The trick is to use see-through plastic templates to center and frame each motif before cutting out the pattern blocks. (For more on clear plastic templates, see page 19).

The crib quilt consists of 30 print blocks and 20 solid blocks set on the diagonal, pieced out with triangles, and framed with narrow bands of fabrics in complementary colors. Both blocks and borders are machine-quilted "in the ditch" (along the seam lines). The plain blocks are embellished with a single hand-quilted heart, and clusters of leaves are quilted in the borders.

The finished quilt measures 36 × 42½ inches.

Materials

Note: Yardages are based on 45-inch fabrics, except where noted.

1 yard 54-inch, floral-patterned chintz (or sufficient yardage to provide thirty 5-inch squares with centered motifs)

1¼ yards green or contrasting solid fabric for solid blocks and outer border strips.

¼ yard *each* of 3 coordinated solid-color fabrics (pink, yellow, and blue) for border strips

1 yard backing fabric

medium-weight batting

clear plastic for templates

Directions

1. Trace the 3 full-size pattern pieces on page 124 and cut matching templates from see-through plastic. (Patterns include ¼-inch seam allowances.)

2. Trace templates on the wrong side of the designated fabrics. Center the design motif *on the diagonal* on each square traced from Template A.

3. Mark and cut the following pieces:

from print fabric:
   (A) 30 blocks with a single motif centered diagonally on each piece

from green (or contrasting solid) fabric:
   (A) 20 blocks
   (B) 18 large triangles
   (C) 4 small triangles
   4 strips, each 2½ × 45 inches, for borders

from each border fabric (pink, blue and yellow):
   4 strips, each 1½ × 45 inches

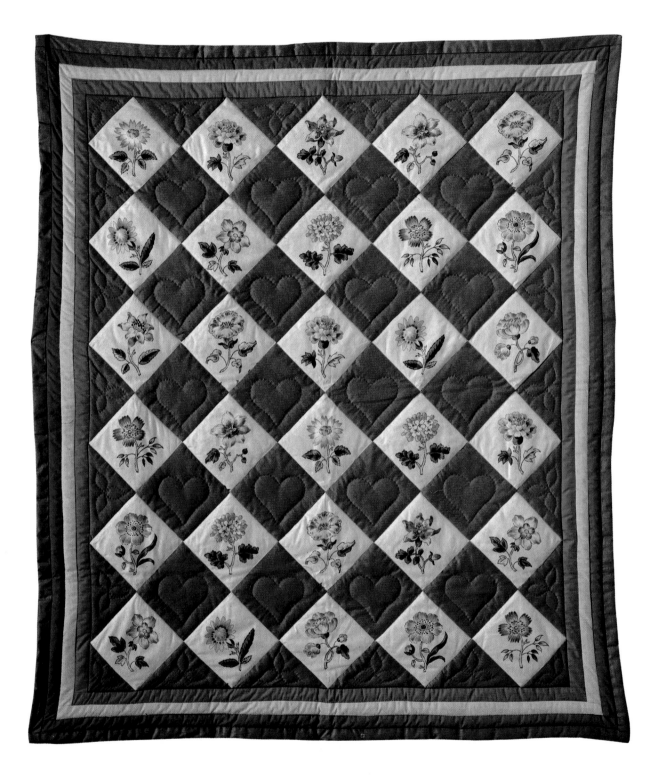

To Assemble the Quilt Top:

1. Arrange print blocks and plain blocks and large and small triangles in diagonal rows, as shown in Figure 1.

2. Beginning in the upper left corner of the quilt top, pin and stitch triangles and squares together to complete each diagonal row of the design as shown in Figure 1, (a) through (l). Use ¼-inch seams throughout. Press the seams open.

3. When all rows are completed, stitch them together to complete quilt top. Pin and stitch 1 pink border strip to each long side and then to the top and bottom of the pieced quilt top (clip the length of strips to size as necessary). Press seams toward border. Repeat for yellow, blue, and then for the wider green strips. Trim the length of each strip as necessary; press seams toward edges.

To Finish the Quilt:

1. Cut the batting and backing 2 inches smaller than the pieced top. Center the top on the batting and baste all 3 layers together.

2. Hand or machine quilt along seam lines of squares and border strips. Trace and quilt a heart on each plain green block. Then quilt clusters of 3 leaves in border triangles and 2 leaves in corner triangles. (See quilting patterns, page 124.)

3. Turn raw edges of the green (outer) border strips under ¼ inch, then fold the border to the back of quilt and pin. Miter the corners and slip-stitch the binding to the backing fabric. (See page 43 for details on self-binding.)

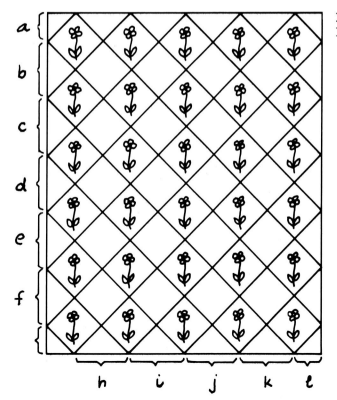

Figure 1. Assembly diagram for Hearts and Flowers crib quilt

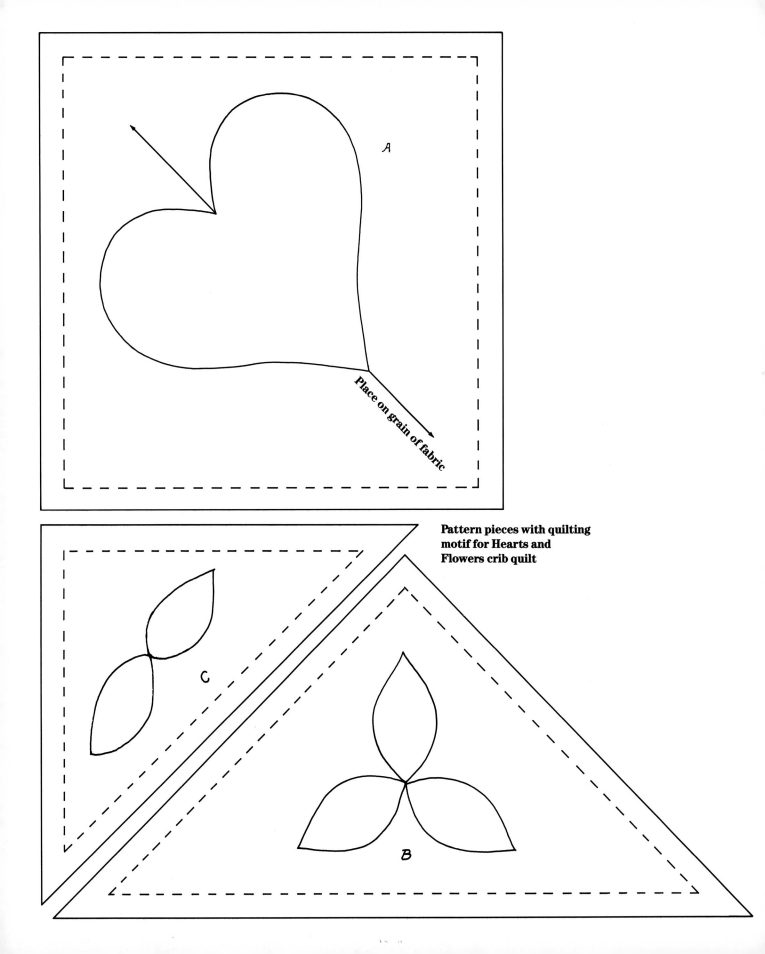

Place on grain of fabric

Pattern pieces with quilting
motif for Hearts and
Flowers crib quilt

A

B

C

LOG CABIN TABLE QUILT

When I found the once-elegant Victorian table quilt shown on page 127 in a Boston thrift shop it was badly damaged, but I fell in love with the pattern and the fabrics. The unusual scalloped border was more or less whole, and the backing was in good shape, so I took a chance and carried home my prize, determined to repair the damage.

The finished piece is hardly an "authentic" restoration — few of us have either the specialized skills or the resources for such an undertaking. I simply tried to retain the flavor of the orginal patchwork by selecting fabrics of similar weight, pattern, and colors for replacement patches.

My refurbished table quilt is still quite fragile, so it hangs on a wall, away from sunlight and home heating units, out of harm's way. You might choose to piece a similar design from jewel-toned velveteens or shiny cotton sateen fabrics, or from any combination of old and new fabric scraps in your collection. The more varied the fabrics in the quilt top, the more interesting the finished design.

The table quilt measures approximately 46 × 46 inches, including the 2¾-inch-wide scalloped border. The design consists of 36 Log Cabin blocks pieced from ¾-inch logs, and the blocks are arranged in 6 rows of 6 blocks each, to form a Light and Dark variation of the Log Cabin pattern.

Materials

Note: Yardage estimates are based on 45-inch-wide fabrics, although for a scrap quilt such as this one, you will use only small amounts of as many different fabrics as possible.

1 yard (total) light-colored fabric scraps, including scraps of gold for the small corner triangles in the border

1 yard (total) dark-colored scraps, including scraps of deep red for the border triangles.

⅜ yard black fabric for block centers and border scallops

1½ yards lightweight muslin backing for squares

5¼ yards narrow black bias binding

1¼ yards backing fabric

cardboard or plastic for templates

Directions

Note: Measurements and pattern pieces include ¼-inch seam allowances.

1. To begin, cut thirty-six 7¼ × 7¼-inch squares of lightweight muslin as the backing for the Log Cabin blocks.

2. Cut thirty-six 1¼-inch squares of black fabric for block centers (piece A in the assembly diagram, Figure 1, page 128). Baste 1 black square to the center of each muslin backing square. (Review basic instructions for the Log Cabin block, pages 19–21.)

3. The fabric "logs" for each block are cut 1¼ inches-wide (¾ inch finished size). Each adjacent pair of logs, (B) and (C), (D) and (E), etc., is cut from the same fabric (see Figure 1). You will need 4 different light and 4 dark fabrics for each block (solid or prints). The selection and arrangement of individual light and dark fabrics never repeats exactly from block to block. Cut a good supply of 1¼-inch-wide strips of any length and divide the strips into piles of light and dark. Pick and choose from these piles as you construct each block, cutting strips to size as the block is constructed.

To Piece One Block

1. For *each* block, cut a total of 16 logs from 8 different fabrics as follows:

from light fabrics:
First fabric: (B) 1¼ × 1¼ inches
(C) 1¼ × 2 inches
Second fabric: (F) 1¼ × 2¾ inches
(G) 1¼ × 3½ inches
Third fabric: (J) 1¼ × 4¼ inches
(K) 1¼ × 5 inches
Fourth fabric: (N) 1¼ × 5¾ inches
(O) 1¼ × 6½ inches

from dark fabrics:
First fabric: (D) 1¼ × 2 inches
(E) 1¼ × 2¾ inches
Second fabric: (H) 1¼ × 3½ inches
(I) 1¼ × 4¼ inches
Third fabric: (L) 1¼ × 5 inches
(M) 1¼ × 5¾ inches
Fourth fabric: (P) 1¼ × 6½ inches
(Q) 1¼ × 7¼ inches

2. Arrange the 16 fabric strips as shown in Figure 1. Stitch the logs in place, using ¼-inch seam.

3. Complete a total of 36 blocks, varying the selection and placement of the light and dark fabrics from block to block.

To Assemble the Quilt Top:

1. Pin and stitch 4 Log Cabin blocks together to form a basic Light and Dark square (see Figure 2). Complete 9 such blocks of 4 squares each, using ¼-inch seams throughout. Press the seams open.

2. Arrange the 9 blocks in 3 rows of 3 blocks each, as shown in Figure 3. Stitch each horizontal row of 3 blocks together; press the seams open. Then pin and stitch the 3 rows of blocks together to form the center of the quilt top. Press the seams open.

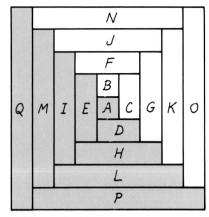

Figure 1. Assembly diagram for one Log Cabin block

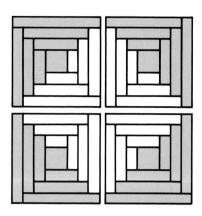

Figure 2. Assembly diagram for 4 Log Cabin blocks

Figure 3. Assembly diagram for Log Cabin quilt top

128

To Piece the Borders:

Note: All pattern pieces include ¼-inch seam allowances.

1. Trace and cut templates for the 5 border pattern pieces on page 131.

2. Cut the following pieces:

    (*R*) 36 triangles from light-colored fabrics

    (*R-1*) 8 triangles from deep-red fabric

    (*S*) 40 scallops from black fabric

    (*T*) Fold black fabric in half; trace and cut 4 of (*T*) from folded fabric, making 8 fabric pieces (4 face up; 4 in reverse)

    (*U*) Fold gold fabric in half; trace and cut 4 (*U*) from folded fabric, making 8 fabric pieces (4 face up; 4 in reverse)

    (*V*) 4 from black fabric

Note: Be sure to keep pattern pieces (*S*), (*T*), and (*V*) in separate stacks, as they are all slightly different sizes of a similar scallop shape and might easily become mixed up.

3. Pin and stitch 1 straight edge of a black scallop (*S*) to 1 side of a large right triangle (*R*). Piece 9 such (*R-S*) units; pin and stitch the 9 (*R-S*) units together to make a border (see Figure 4). Press the seams open.

4. For the *right* end of the border (with scallops pointing toward you and straight edge pointing away from you): Pin and stitch 1 red triangle (*R-1*) to a large black scallop (*S*) and one small gold triangle (*U*) to a smaller black scallop (*T*), as shown in Figure 5. Pin and stitch these 2 units together and then join the pieced unit to the right end of the pieced border strip. Press the seams open.

5. For the *left* end of border, pin and stitch together a red triangle (*R-1*), a smaller black scallop (*T*), and a small gold triangle (*U*), as shown in Figure 6. Pin and stitch this pieced unit to the left end of border. Press the seams open.

6. Make 4 border strips as described in steps 3–5 above. Pin and stitch the long straight edge of 1 border to 1 side of the pieced Log Cabin top. Pin and stitch a second border strip to the opposite side. Press the seams toward the center of the quilt.

7. To complete the top and bottom borders, stitch 1 of the 4 remaining black scallops (*V*) to each end of the 2 remaining border strips. Pin and stitch the completed borders to the top and bottom of the quilt. Press seams toward the center of the quilt.

To Piece the Backing:

1. Cut a square of backing fabric slightly larger than the pieced Log Cabin center of the quilt (approximately 41 × 41 inches). Using ¼-inch seams, pin and stitch a 3½-inch-wide strip of backing fabric to each of the 4 sides of the backing square. Press the seams toward the edges.

2. With *wrong* sides facing, pin the pieced backing square to the Log Cabin top, matching border seams in the pieced backing to border seams on the quilt top. Baste. Trim the edges of the backing fabric to match the scalloped border on top. Topstitch together the border and the backing ⅛ inch in from the scalloped edge.

To Finish the Quilt:

1. Tie the pieced top and the backing fabric together at the corner points of each Log Cabin block (see page 40 for tips on tying a quilt).

2. Bind the raw edges of the scalloped border with narrow strips of black bias tape (refer to page 43 for details).

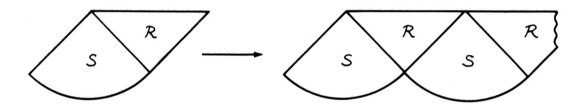

Figure 4. Piecing the border

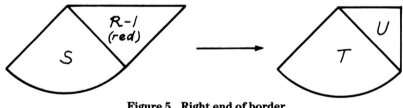

Figure 5. Right end of border

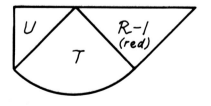

Figure 6. Left end of border

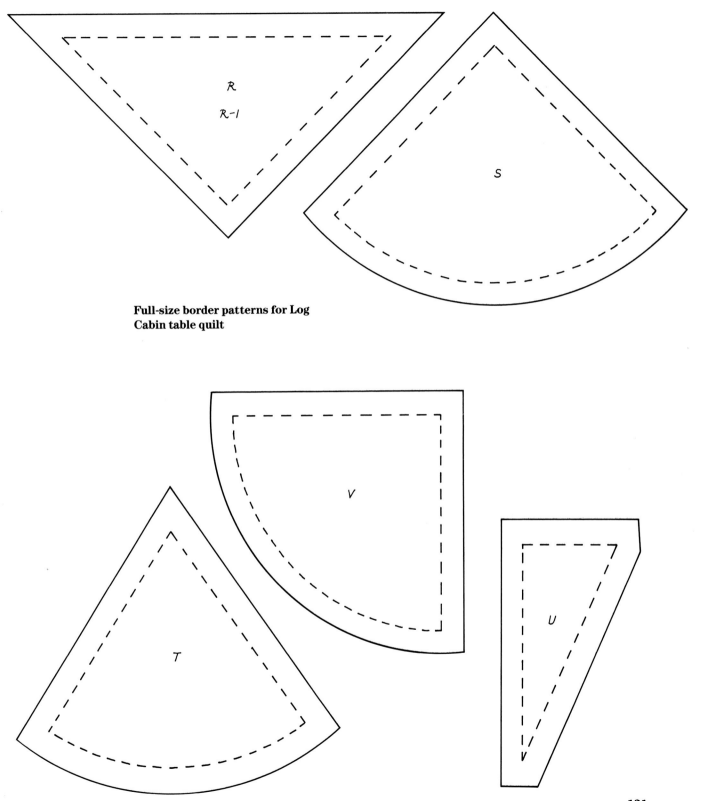

**Full-size border patterns for Log
Cabin table quilt**

R

R-1

S

V

T

U

131

THE WANDERER QUILT

Rocky Road to Jericho, Baby Bunting, and Cleopatra's Puzzle are among the other names for this intricately pieced design. In view of how this particular quilt came to be made, however, I prefer the old Victorian pattern name: The Wanderer.

The little fan blocks from which the quilt is pieced were given to me by a California friend while we were visiting mutual friends in North Carolina. The Californian had discoverd them at the bottom of a trunk she had recently purchased during a vacation in Vermont. I have no idea who began the project — or where — but suddenly I found myself with over 300 pieced and partially pieced fan squares stuffed in a paper bag, just waiting to be put to use!

Some of the squares had been pieced by hand, others by machine, and the quality of the stitching was uneven at best. It seems clear that at least 2 different people, perhaps more, had worked on this quilt in the past. Were they mother and daughter? A neighborhood sewing circle? I will never know, but once the pieces were entrusted to me, I felt obliged to complete this cooperative venture.

Having no notion of the original piecemakers' intended design, I happily experimented with a number of different block settings before deciding on the one you see here. The results of those early experiments — a selection of smaller projects, using fan squares in a variety of arrangements — appear on pages 74–80. There you will also find full-size patterns and directions for piecing the basic fan block.

The Wanderer quilt consists of 144 pieced 5-inch squares arranged in 9 large pattern blocks of 16 squares each. The blocks are set in 3 rows of 3 large blocks each, with a 1-block-wide border. The pieced design is framed with 3-inch-wide strips of red-print fabric and bound with a narrow band of lilac. Each fan block is outline quilted, as are the borders. The finished size of the quilt is 77 × 77 inches.

Materials

Note: Yardages are based on 45-inch-wide fabrics.

⅞ yard lilac fabric (Template A)
4 yards (total) assorted print fabrics (Template B)
3¼ yards white fabric (Template C)
4¼ yards backing fabric (white or lilac or small floral print)
1 yard red-print fabric for borders
9 yards wide lilac bias binding
lightweight batting
clear plastic printed with a grid, for templates

Directions

Note: All pattern pieces and measurements include ¼-inch seam allowances.

1. Turn to page 81 for patterns. Trace the 3 pattern pieces for the fan block and transfer to clear plastic to make templates. Take special care to accurately mark and cut notches on templates (A) and (C).

2. Referring to the basic directions for making fan blocks given on pages 74–75, cut and stitch a total of 196 fan blocks. Press all seams toward the lilac corner of each block, piece (A).

3. Trace and cut a 5-inch square of clear plastic. Center the square on the wrong side of each pieced fan block and trace around the square to mark stitching lines as described in step 6 on page 75.

To Assemble One Wanderer Pattern Block:

1. Arrange 16 small pieced fan blocks in 4 horizontal rows of 4 squares each, as shown in Figure 1. With right sides facing, pin and stitch the 4 squares of each row together, taking care to match the marked seam lines as accurately as possible. Press the seams.

2. Pin and stitch Rows 1, 2, 3, and 4 together, matching the seam lines. Press the block.

3. Complete 9 large pattern blocks as described in Steps 1 and 2 above. Set aside.

To Assemble Quilt Borders:

1. To piece 1 side border, pin and stitch 12 fan squares in a row, as shown in Figure 2. Press the border. Repeat for the second side border.

2. For the top border, pin and stitch 14 fan squares together, as shown in Figure 3. Repeat for the bottom border. Press.

To Assemble the Quilt Top:

1. Arrange the 9 pieced pattern blocks in 3 rows of 3 blocks each. Pin and stitch the blocks of each row together, matching the seams carefully. Use ¼-inch seams throughout.

2. Now pin and stitch the 3 rows of blocks together, matching the seams, to form the center of the quilt top. Press.

3. Pin and stitch side borders on either side of center, then pin and stitch the top and bottom borders in place. Press.

4. Cut and piece 2 strips of red-print fabric, each 3½ × 70 inches. Pin and stitch 1 of these border strips to each side of the quilt top. Cut and piece 2 strips of red-print fabric, each 3½ × 76¼ inches. Pin and stitch 1 strip to the top and 1 to the bottom of the quilt. Press seams toward the red borders.

To Finish the Quilt:

1. Press the quilt top gently on wrong side.

2. Piece the backing fabric to size (approximately 77 × 77 inches).

3. Layer the backing, batting, and pieced quilt top together, pin and baste through all 3 layers.

4. Outline quilt ¼ inch beyond all seam lines on each fan square, or quilt as desired. See page 37 for details on quilting.

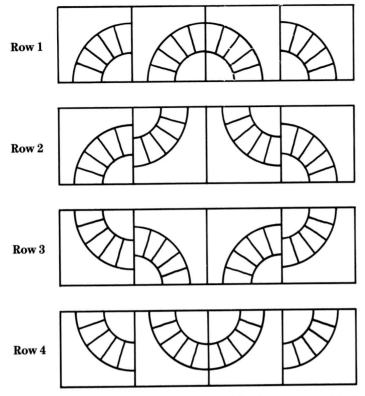

Row 1

Row 2

Row 3

Row 4

Figure 1. Assembly diagram for Wanderer pattern block

Figure 2. Side borders

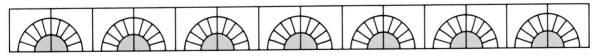

Figure 3. Top and bottom borders

135

5. Remove the basting; trim batting and backing even with edges of the pieced top. Bind the edges of the quilt with wide lilac bias binding.

PEACEFUL STAR QUILT

Stitched from soft floral prints in pastel shades, with just a touch of dark-blue print to give the pattern punch, this handsome king-size spread is pieced and quilted entirely by machine. The mix of small-, medium-, and large-scale prints, and the artful combination of a pieced center medallion with curved borders and appliquéd swags creates a wonderfully lyrical design reminiscent of nineteenth-century chintz coverlets and yet thoroughly contemporary at the same time. Curves in the pattern are highlighted with narrow strips of bias binding stitched along the corner and border pieces, further softening the design. The scale-down pattern assembly diagram on page 139 will enable you to draft the necessary pattern templates for the Peaceful Star quilt. Also included are full-size patterns for the appliquéd border swags, as these curved shapes are a bit difficult to draft freehand.

The finished quilt measures 90 × 96 inches.

Materials

Six different fabrics are used for the quilt — 2 each in small-, medium-, and large-scale designs. Because the pattern shapes are large, particularly the corner and border shapes, the yardage estimates given below (based on 45-inch-wide fabrics) are generous enough to allow you to cut each pattern shape and border strip without having to piece the fabric. There will be some fabric left over, which might be used to make companion projects, such as pillows, if you wish.

Note: In the following materials list and in the directions, fabrics are identified by capital letters and pattern pieces are identified by numbers.

(A) ¾ yard large-scale peach and green print
(B) 1⅔ yards medium-scale dark-blue print
(C) ⅓ yard small-scale pale-green print
(D) 2 yards large-scale blue/gold/pale-yellow print
(E) 5 yards medium-scale peach on pale-blue background print
(F) 2½ yards small-scale pale-peach print
5½ yards backing fabric (or king-size sheet)
90 × 96-inch piece of polyester batting
plastic or cardboard for templates
graph paper and brown wrapping paper for drafting patterns

Directions

1. Refer to Figure 1 on page 139. Enlarge quilt pattern to size and transfer to brown paper (tape sheets of paper together if necessary). See page 8 for details on enlarging patterns.

2. Trace and cut plastic or cardboard templates for pattern pieces 1–4; make brown paper patterns for pieces 5–8.

   Note: Border pieces 7 and 8 are both cut whole; swag strips pieced from shapes 9 and 10 are appliquéd on top of these border strips.

   Add ¼-inch seam allowances to all templates and paper patterns.

3. *For pattern piece 5:* Cut the outer edge as a straight line, as indicated by the dotted line on the pattern; mark the curved edge as a stitching line only.

   For pattern piece 6: Cut the diagonal edge of the triangle along the scallop as indicated but cut the sides as straight edges, as shown by the dotted lines on the pattern; mark curved edges as stitching lines only.

4. Trace and cut templates for border swag (pieces 9 and 10) from the full-size patterns on page 142. Add ¼-inch seam allowances to each piece.

5. Trace and cut the following patterns from the fabrics indicated (all pieces should be traced on wrong side of fabric):

   (*A*) 4 of Template 1

   (*B*) 8 of Template 2, 4 of Template 6, and 28 of Template 9

   (*C*) 8 of Template 3

   (*D*) 4 of Template 4 and 4 of Template 5

   (*E*) 2 of the top and bottom border Template 7 and 2 of side border Template 8 (piece 7 is slightly wider than piece 8)

   (*F*) 28 of Template 10; cut and piece 12 yards 1½-inch-wide bias strips and 10 yards 2½-inch bias strips (see page 43 for details on cutting bias strips.)

To Assemble the Quilt Top:

1. Using ¼-inch seams throughout, piece the center block of the quilt top as shown in Figure 2, page 140. First piece 2 of Row B and 1 of Row C. Stitch 1 triangle (Row A) atop each B unit, then piece 1 B unit to each side of Row C. Press the seams carefully.

2. Cut a piece of 1½-inch-wide bias fabric (*F*) about 40 inches long. Press edges in toward the center, ¼ inch along each side of the strip. Fold the strip in half lengthwise and press; pin and stitch the bias binding over the scalloped edge of one corner piece 6. Repeat for the 3 remaining corner pieces.

3. Lap the bound edge of 1 corner (piece 6) over the matching edge of 1 strip (piece 5). Topstitch piece 5 to piece 6 along the inner edge of the bias binding. Repeat for 3 remaining corners.

4. Pin and stitch 1 pieced corner unit (pieces 5 and 6) to each side of the pieced center square (¼-inch seams).

5. Prepare 1½-inch-wide bias strips of fabric *F* as described in step 2 above and bind the scalloped edges of the top and bottom border pieces (Template 7).

Each square equals 3 inches
Dotted lines indicate where pattern pieces overlap

Figure 1. Pattern and assembly diagram for Peaceful Star quilt

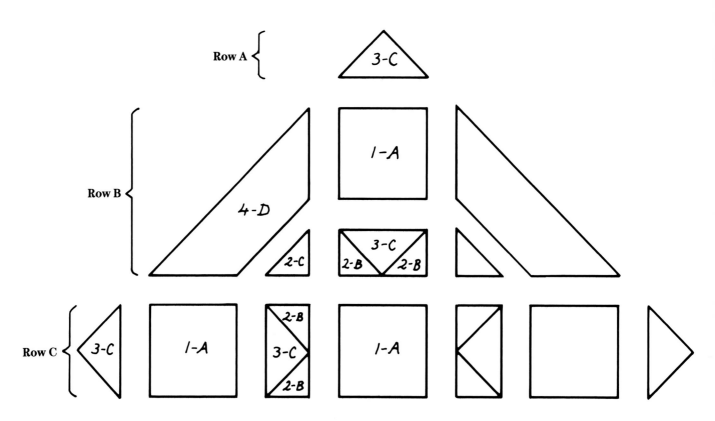

Figure 2. Assembly diagram for center block of Peaceful Star quilt

Pin and topstitch the top and bottom borders in place. Repeat the procedure for the side borders (piece 8), mitering the seam where border strips 7 and 8 meet at the corners.

For Appliqué Border Swag:

1. For each top and bottom border: Pin and stitch 6 of piece 9 and 7 of piece 10 together, matching the dots at points *A* and *B* and alternating the shapes to reproduce the scalloped border shown on the pattern. Begin and end each swag with a piece 10. Press.

2. For side borders, piece 9 of piece 9 and 7 of piece 10 together, alternating the shapes to form the scallop swag described above. Begin and end each swag with a piece 9. Press.

3. Clip the curves and seam allowances. Baste under the ¼-inch seam allowance on all swags and position swags on the borders of the quilt top, matching corners as shown in Figure 1. Pin and stitch all swags in place (appliqué swags by hand or machine topstitch, as desired).

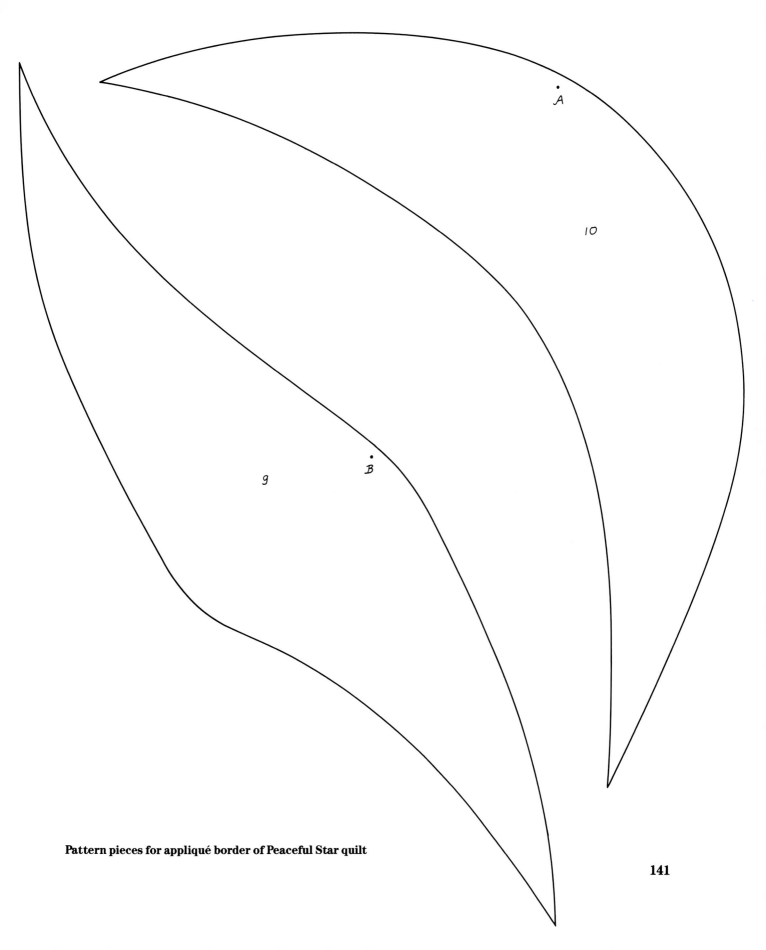

A

10

B

9

Pattern pieces for appliqué border of Peaceful Star quilt

To Complete the Quilt:

1. Piece the backing to size (approximately 90 × 96 inches).

2. Layer the backing, batting, and pieced top together and baste.

3. Machine quilt "in the ditch" along all seam lines. Also quilt about 3 inches in from the seam lines on the larger pieces to secure the batting and to add texture to the surface of the quilt.

4. Bind the raw edges of the quilt with 2½-inch-wide bias-cut strips of fabric (F).

INDEX

For information on how you can have
Better Homes and Gardens
delivered to your door, write to:
Mr. Robert Austin,
P.O. Box 4536, Des Moines, IA 50336